Video Games and the Law

The video game industry is big business, not only in terms of the substantial revenue generated through retail sales of games themselves, but also in terms of the size and value of parallel and secondary markets. Consider any popular video game today, and you most likely are looking at a franchise that includes not only the game itself and all of its variants, but also toys, books, movies, and more, with legions of fans that interact with the industry in myriad ways. Surveying the legal landscape of this emergent industry, Ron Gard and Elizabeth Townsend-Gard shed light on the many important topics where law is playing an important role. In examining these issues, *Video Games and the Law* is both a legal and a cultural look at the development of the video game industry and the role that law has played so far in this industry's ability to thrive and grow.

Ron Gard is Director of the Law/Culture/Innovation Initiative and teaches in the Communication department at Tulane University. He is a Non-Resident Fellow at Stanford University's Center for Internet and Society.

Elizabeth Townsend Gard is the Jill. H and Avram A. Glazer Professor in Social Entrepreneurship at Tulane University, Director of the Tulane Center for IP, Media & Culture, and teaches intellectual property at Tulane Law School.

Video Games and the Law

Video Games and the Law

**Ron Gard and
Elizabeth Townsend Gard**

with contributions from John Billiris,
Karl Craig, Mark Donatiello, Markeecha
Forcell, Kelvin Lai, Mitchell Longan, and
Alexandra Stork

Routledge
Taylor & Francis Group

LONDON AND NEW YORK

First published 2017 by Routledge

2 Park Square, Milton Park, Abingdon, Oxfordshire OX14 4RN
52 Vanderbilt Avenue, New York, NY 10017

Routledge is an imprint of the Taylor & Francis Group, an informa business

First issued in paperback 2020

Copyright © 2017 Taylor & Francis

Library of Congress Cataloging-in-Publication Data
Names: Gard, Ron, author. | Townsend Gard, Elizabeth, author.
Title: Video games and the law / Ron Gard and Elizabeth
  Townsend Gard ; with contributions from John Billiris,
  Karl Craig, Mark Donatiello, Markeecha Forcell,
  Kelvin Lai, Mitchell Longan, and Alexandra Stork.
Description: New York : Routledge, 2017.
Identifiers: LCCN 2016050413 | ISBN 9781138630765 (hardback) |
  ISBN 9781315209210 (ebk)
Subjects: LCSH: Video games—Law and legislation—United States.
Classification: LCC KF3994 .G37 2017 | DDC 344.73/099—dc23
LC record available at https://lccn.loc.gov/2016050413

ISBN: 978-1-138-63076-5 (hbk)
ISBN: 978-0-367-60744-9 (pbk)

Typeset in Times New Roman
by Apex CoVantage, LLC

Contents

Author Biographies

Ron Gard holds a PhD in English with an emphasis in Cultural Studies and a JD from the University of Arizona. He has taught at Tulane University, University of New Orleans, University of Arizona, and California State University Northridge. He is a licensed attorney in New York. At Tulane University, he divides his time teaching film, media, and social theory courses in the Communication Department; entrepreneurship in the Social Innovation Social Entrepreneurship minor program; and running the Law/Culture/Innovation Initiative. He is the CEO of Limited Times, LLC, and is a nonresident fellow at Stanford Law School's Center for Internet and Society. He is co-investigator on the Role of Law as Creativity Project, which has been interviewing industry leaders in Los Angeles, Seattle, New York, and other cities to better understand the relationship between doctrines of law and practice in the content industry in the twenty-first century.

Elizabeth Townsend Gard is an Associate Professor of Law and the Jill H. and Avram A. Professor of Social Entrepreneurship at Tulane University, with a specialty in copyright law. Her main project for the last decade has been the Durationator Copyright Resource, a software tool that assists lawyers and nonlawyers alike in determining the copyright status of any kind of work—e.g., a poem, a song, a movie—anywhere in the world. She began her copyright quest while earning a PhD in European history at UCLA. She received a JD and LLM from the University of Arizona and was awarded a postdoc at the London School of Economics. She has written papers on the subjects of Pinterest, Second Life, podcasts, and other emerging areas of copyright law.

Acknowledgments

A special thanks to Judd Ruggill and Ken McAllister, whose work on video games served as the genesis of this book. A genuine thanks also to those who gave so generously of their time for interviews and helped shape our perspectives on this subject matter. These include Don McGowan, General Counsel, The Pokémon Company; J. Michael Monahan, Astrolabe, LLC; Matthew Skelton, Senior Attorney, Legal & Corporate Affairs, Microsoft; Kevin Reilly, Sony; Patrick Sweeney, IE Law Group and founder of the Video Game Bar Association; Betsy Rosenblatt, attorney and professor of law; David Levine, professor of law; and Jana McDougall, Sony Interactive Entertainment. Thanks also to the students in the Advanced Copyright course in the spring of 2016 at Tulane Law School, without whom this book would not have come to be. Some of these individuals became contributors to the work, and their names are credited as such. Thanks to Alexandra Stork for her work refining the project and editorially assisting with the book and to Corey Friedman for reviewing the manuscript in its last steps.

1 Introduction[1]

In the summer of 2016, a new phenomenon appeared literally in the streets around the world: *Pokémon Go*.[2] Played on a mobile device, the game combines the virtual reality of the beloved Pokémon characters with the real world, sending players on a quest, far and wide, to "catch them all."[3] People sought out Pokémon in parks, shops, restaurants, and even the U.S. Holocaust Museum.[4] The app made widely evident what already has been true for some time—video games have moved well beyond gaming consoles within our homes to now occupy a broader, more significant place within our social environment.

As the presence of video games has grown, notably so, too, have the legal issues to which they have given rise. If intellectual property concerns, such as copyright or trademark protection, at one time dominated this field, no longer do those concerns mark the limits of legal contemplations. *Pokémon Go*, for example, has raised issues such as trespass onto property, as individuals in pursuit of capturing Pokémon entered the yards of private homes.[5] There were even news reports of armed robbers using the game to "lure players into a trap."[6] Likely most revealing in regard to the significance of video game development and the legal issues accompanying it, however, were the spate of stories regarding new business opportunities that *Pokémon Go* made possible. A *Forbes* article, titled "How to Ride the *Pokémon Go* Wave to Business Success," explained how small businesses could increase traffic by engaging in *Pokémon Go* marketing by creating a "Pokémon Lure Module purchase for the physical retail location," Pokémon Gyms, and eventually paid sponsorship opportunities.[7]

The economic impact of *Pokémon Go* in the summer of 2016 could not be missed. Media headlines blared statements such as: "Nintendo is now worth more than Sony thanks to *Pokémon Go*."[8] The accompanying article makes clear just what an economic juggernaut *Pokémon Go* proved to be:

> Pokémon, whoa. Nintendo is now worth more than double what it was before the launch of *Pokémon Go*, as investors continue to drive up the

price of the video game company's stock. In dollar terms, Nintendo has added a whopping $23 billion to its value in less than two weeks. The share price increase has sent Nintendo's market capitalization—the value of the company based on its stock price—to more than $40 billion. That's more than one of its rivals in the video game industry, Sony, which is around $38 billion.[9]

Before *Pokémon Go*, when one thought of video games, one likely thought primarily of the devices on which games are played—originally, arcade cabinets; then home gaming consoles and computers; and, most recently, smartphones. This expansion in means of play, however, is indicative of a more significant, if less apparent, expansion. For all its ingenuity, *Pokémon Go* proves in many respects to be not so much a new phenomenon, but in fact just another step in the integration of game play into the material environment around us. This book explores a particular dimension of that integration: the legal landscape of video games. Two major factors influence the relationship of the law and video games: (1) user-generated interactions and (2) the expansion of what the "video game" industry is into multilayered approaches to product and brand expansion. Take any video game—*Pac-Man*,[10] *Call of Duty*,[11] *World of Warcraft*.[12] Each of these works is protected by the law in a number of ways—copyright, trademark, patents, employment laws, contracts, and trade secrets, to name the most basic. This book considers issues emergent in the relationship of the law to the video game industry. While the book's focus is on U.S. law, many of the issues addressed evince global and international dimensions.

Throughout video gaming's history, questions have arisen as to what rights game and game system companies have over their creations, including whether or not they have the right to exclude third parties from creating hardware and software to use with their licensed gaming devices. As video games have become more prolific in society, an entire fan-based culture has developed around them, involving the creation of permitted and unlicensed fan works both for profit and not for profit.[13] The video game industry was the first to embrace their fans and see their activities as an asset rather than an assault. In other instances, third-party companies have created unlicensed hardware to use with gaming platforms against the wishes of the platform's creator. Websites such as YouTube and even the game platforms themselves[14] make it easier than ever for people to upload videos of themselves playing, commenting on, and reviewing games, often using content from the games in the videos. 'Let's Play' videos have become a popular form of entertainment over the past few years, and some of the creators of those videos even profit from them. Websites such as Etsy make it easy for fans to create and sell unlicensed video game–themed merchandise.[15] And as of

2016, at least five universities have League of Legends teams that include video game scholarships to play in eSports tournaments.[16] These sorts of uses implicate a number of laws, as well as company policies, regarding the enforcement of laws or the allowance of permissible uses. And then, of course, there are the troublemakers and naughty behaviors like swatting that are tied to the video game industry.[17]

Over the past twenty years, the video game world has evolved from a small, boutique-style marketplace into one that has become one of the biggest players in the entertainment industry.[18] According to consulting firm Price Waterhouse Coopers (PWC), the global video game industry grossed $56 billion in revenue in 2011.[19] In just one day, sales for Activision's *Call of Duty: Black Ops 2*[20] soared past the all-time opening box-office record set by Disney's *The Avengers*[21] by more than $300 million.[22] PWC predicted that video games will be the fastest-growing form of media over the next few years, with sales rising to $82 billion by 2016.[23] The *Call of Duty* franchise has topped $10 billion in lifetime revenue, substantially more than any film franchise ever.[24] Video games are transforming the entertainment industry, and the need to provide modernized intellectual property protection, particularly through adaptive copyright law measures, has become increasingly apparent.[25]

While traditional topics, such as copyright law, surrounding legal protection of video games as properties remain important, the legal world of video games rapidly has expanded. The legal issues of the video game industry have become fairly complex and broad. We heard this from everyone who we interviewed, but it was underscored by Matt Skelton, an attorney at Microsoft who oversees the *Halo*[26] franchise. Skelton is an attorney in Microsoft's Entertainment and Devices Division, more specifically in the Xbox division that includes *Minecraft*,[27] *Halo*, eSports, and *Gears of War*,[28] along with other titles. He specifically focuses his time on *Halo* and *Gears of War*. He described his job as mostly "bread and butter IP issues, software development, and licensing issues." He also finds himself doing employment issues, nondisclosure agreements, noncompete agreements, and other general legal issues. Skelton described his job as a combination of legal issues that would arise at a motion picture studio, but with the additional issues of a commercial software publisher.

He described three areas of commercialization and product development that occur with a property like *Halo*. First, there is the consumer product/licensing team, with about fifty consumer product licensees with the *Halo* brand. A dedicated team reviews product prototypes on a full-time basis. These are specialists from different fields—literature, for example (there are nineteen novels based on *Halo*, with eight making it to the best-seller list). Then, there is the team working on original content, not only on new video games, but short stories, live action episodes, and animation series.

Third, there is eSports, which has grown into competitions with sometimes millions in prize money. All three activities require a tremendous amount of legal work and sorting through issues that arise.

Another property, *Skylanders*, crossed the $1 billion revenue mark in 2013, with over 100 million toys sold, the toys being a necessary component of the game.[29] That was only two years after its debut in 2011. "The Skylanders franchise became the first kids' video game intellectual property to cross the $1 billion mark in just 15 months, and I think we are still just starting to realize its potential."[30] By 2016, sales had reached $3 billion and 250 million toys sold, even with new competition from Disney ($1 billion in sales) and Legos.[31]

The range of legal issues examined herein is wide in scope, affecting game creators and game players alike. Chapter 2, "Copyright and Video Games," looks in some depth at copyright issues as they have evolved in the industry in recent decades. Chapter 3, "Legal Issues beyond Copyright," looks further than copyright matters to consider legal issues such as patents, trademarks, contracts, and First Amendment questions. Chapter 4, "The Gaming Community and Fans," focuses on legal issues involving fan uses, including fan fiction, fan labor, and doxing and swatting. Chapter 5, "Employment," considers legal issues facing video game employees in the employment law context. Chapter 6, "Legal Issues with eSports," takes up legal matters arising in the financially booming field of eSports. Chapter 7, "Conclusion: The New Normal," returns to the recent *Pokémon Go* phenomenon to consider legal issues in the aggregate and into the future as they appear presently from the emergent intersection of the virtual and the terrestrial.

Notes

1. John Billiris contributed to the writing of this chapter.
2. *Pokémon Go*. Niantic. Niantic, 2016. iOS, Android, Apple Watch.
3. Jacobsson Purewal, Sarah. "*Pokémon Go* FAQ: The Beginner's Guide on How to Catch 'em All." *Macworld*, 22 August 2016, http://www.macworld.com/article/3094801/software-games/the-beginner-s-guide-to-pok-mon-go-an-faq-on-how-to-catch-em-all.html.
4. Peterson, Andrea. "Holocaust Museum to Visitors: Please Stop Catching Pokémon Here." *Washington Post*, 12 July 2016, https://www.washingtonpost.com/news/the-switch/wp/2016/07/12/holocaust-museum-to-visitors-please-stop-catching-pokemon-here/.
5. "Teen Killed Trespassing while Playing *Pokémon Go*." *National Report*, http://nationalreport.net/teen-killed-trespassing-while-playing-pokemon-go/.
6. "*Pokémon Go*: Armed Robbers Use Mobile Game to Lure Players into Trap." *The Guardian*, https://www.theguardian.com/technology/2016/jul/10/pokemon-go-armed-robbers-dead-body.

7. "How to Ride the *Pokémon Go* Wave to Business Success." *Forbes*, 22 July 2016, http://www.forbes.com/sites/quora/2016/07/22/how-to-ride-the-pokemon-wave-to-business-success/—555e1c632063.

8. Abbruzzese, Jason. "Nintendo Is Now Worth More than Sony Thanks to *Pokémon Go*." 19 July 2016, http://mashable.com/2016/07/19/nintendo-worth-more-than-sony/#BtoCUlc7zuqW: "The game itself was developed by Niantic, a private company that spun out of Google. The Pokémon characters are property of The Pokémon Company. Nintendo has a partial ownership stake in both those companies, meaning they'll get a cut of the game's success."

9. Ibid.

10. *Pac-Man*. Namco. Midway, 1980. Arcade game.

11. *Call of Duty*. Infinity Ward. Activision, 2003. Multiple platforms.

12. *World of Warcraft*. Blizzard Entertainment. Blizzard Entertainment, 2004. Multiple platforms.

13. "In certain games, fans of the game have built entire online communities dedicated to creating and sharing user-generated content, which can be downloaded and incorporated into the game. For example, fans of Electronic Arts' *The Sims* series, can go to "The Sims Resource" and other similar sites to download custom user-generated content to modify their virtual families and towns." *The Sims Resource*. N.p., n.d. Web. 03 Mar. 2016.

14. "Record Game Clips with Game DRV," http://support.xbox.com/en-US/xbox-one/apps/upload-game-dvr. Marinconz, Steve. "How to Capture Video Game Footage on PS4, Xbox One, PC and Mac." *Kotaku*, 18 November 2014, http://kotaku.com/how-to-capture-game-video-on-ps4-xbox-one-pc-and-mac-1659764485; Schneider, Steven. "How to Record Video Games on PC and Consoles." *Tech Time*, 08 June 2016, http://www.techtimes.com/articles/163631/20160608/how-to-record-video-games-on-pc-and-consoles.htm.

15. "Etsy—Your Place to Buy and Sell All Things Handmade, Vintage, and Supplies." *Etsy*. N.p., n.d. Web. 03 Mar. 2016.

16. "At Least 5 Colleagues Now Have League of Legends, Esports Scholarships." *Daily Dot*, 05 November 2015, http://www.dailydot.com/esports/league-of-legends-college-scholarships/. Even *Time* magazine ran an article: Gregory, Sean. "America's First Video Game Varsity Athletes." *Time*, 27 March 2015, http://time.com/3756140/video-games-varsity/. See also, "25 Great Scholarships for Gamers." *Top 10 Online Colleges*, http://www.top10onlinecolleges.org/scholarships-for/gamers/

17. The Urban Dictionary defines swatting as: "a goal achieved by hacking where the hacker tricks 911 systems into deploying SWAT to an unsuspecting victim's home under false pretenses." *Urban Dictionary*, http://www.urbandictionary.com/define.php?term=swatting. Usually this is when an unsuspecting gamer is streaming live so that the SWAT team arriving is captured by viewers. "15 Year Old Who "SWATTED" Gamer Convicted of Domestic Terrorism; 25 Years to Life in Federal Prison." *National Report*, http://nationalreport.net/15-year-old-swatted-domestic-terrorism/.

18. "Shoot 'em Up." *The Economist*. N.p., December 2011. Web. http://www.economist.com/blogs/graphicdetail/2011/12/daily-chart-0. "All of the 11 Biggest Video Game Companies in the World That You're about to See Have Watched Gaming Go Mainstream and Turn into One of the Largest Branches of the Entertainment Industry and Also One of the Fastest Growing." *Insider Monkey*, 19

June 2015, "11 Biggest Video Game Companies in the World." http://www.insi dermonkey.com/blog/11-biggest-video-game-companies-in-the-world-354814/

19. Ibid.
20. *Call of Duty: Black Ops 2*. Treyarch. Activision, 2012. Windows.
21. *The Avengers*. Dir. Joss Whedon. Marvel Studios/Paramount Pictures, 2012. Film.
22. Corliss, Ricard. "Beyond Marvel-ous: The Avengers Smashes Records with $200.3 Million." *Time.com*, 06 May 2012. Web. 03 Mar. 2016, http://enter tainment.time.com/2012/05/06/beyond-marvel-ous-the-avengers-smashes-records-with-200-3-million/
23. Ibid.
24. Makuch, Eddie. "Call of Duty: Advanced Warfare Labeled "Biggest Entertain-ment Launch of 2014." *GameSpot*. Gamespot, 20 November 2014. Web. 03 Mar. 2016, http://www.gamespot.com/articles/call-of-duty-advanced-warfare-labeled-biggest-ente/1100–6423717/
25. Chang, Steve, and Ross Dannenberg. "Hey, That's MY Game! Intellectual Prop-erty Protection for Video Games." *Gamasutra Article*. Gamasutra, 25 Febru-ary 2008. Web. 03 Mar. 2016, http://www.gamasutra.com/view/feature/3546/hey_thats_my_game_intellectual_.php?print=1.
26. *Halo* (franchise). Bungie/Ensemble Studios/343 Industries/Creative Assembly. Microsoft Studios, 2001–2015. Multiple platforms.
27. *Minecraft* (franchise). Mojang/4J Studios/Microsoft Studios. Mojang/Microsoft Studios/Sony Computer Entertainment, 2011–2015. Multiple platforms.
28. *Gears of War* (franchise). Epic Games/The Coalition. Microsoft Studios, 2006–2016.
29. Grubb, Jeff. "Skylanders Crosses the $1B Revenue Mark with Over 100M Toys Sold." *Venture Beat*, 11 February 2013, http://venturebeat.com/2013/02/11/skylanders-crosses-the-1b-revenue-mark-with-over-100m-toys-sold/
30. Ibid., quote from Activision Publishing chief executive officer Eric Hirshberg.
31. Morris, Chris. "Rough Skies May Be Ahead for Activision's Skylanders." *CNBC*, 14 June 2016, http://www.cnbc.com/2016/06/14/rough-skies-may-be-ahead-for-activisions-skylanders.html.

2 Copyright and Video Games[1]

What Is Copyright?

For video games and the various products created around them, copyright law serves traditionally as the legal basis for protecting the creations—the game itself, books pertaining to the games, dolls of characters from the game, etc. Trademark, of course, protects the brand, and patent may protect the hardware associated with the game. But copyright is the heart of the protection of the creative expression itself.[2]

Copyright law is the main law in the United States and around the world that protects creative, artistic, and written works. This includes books, audiovisual works, art works, computer programs, sound recordings, performances, and broadcasts. Not every country protects video games in exactly the same way under copyright. In 2013, the World Intellectual Property Organization (WIPO) issued a paper titled "The Legal Status of Video Games: Comparative Analysis in National Approaches," which compared the different approaches to copyright of videos games across various countries.[3] It described video games as "complex works of authorship—containing multiple art forms, such as music, scripts, plots, video, paintings and characters—that involve human interaction while executing the game with a computer program on specific hardware."[4] Some aspects of game-related intellectual property are governed by patent law or trademark law,[5] whereas functional elements of console and game design may not be eligible for copyright protection, and even creative elements' copyrights may be limited by jurisdiction.[6]

This chapter will set out the basics of how copyright works and in what instances copyright issues have arisen in the video game industry. Chapter 4 will look at gamer and fan-related matters, which also give rise to copyright issues.

The game itself (the code, the images, the story, etc.) are protected by copyright law—both in the United States and around the world—from the moment the work is created and for decades thereafter. In the United States, the term of protection is generally 95 years from publication.[7] Some components of the game—elements that every game needs—are not protected.[8] Copyright has mechanisms to assure that everyone can use standard mechanisms.[9]

Not all subject matter is protected by copyright. Methods or rules of games, for example, are not protected. When video games were first created, the courts were unsure whether they met the established subject matter requirement under copyright law. Initially, the Copyright Office and a district court judge did not believe so. In *Atari Games v. Oman*,[10] both found that Atari's *Breakout*[11] was merely sounds and geometric shapes and did not rise to the level of creativity required. This holding subsequently was overturned in *Atari Games v. Oman*,[12] where Judge Ruth Bader Ginsburg found the video game analogous to audiovisual works. On a separate basis, however, the Copyright Office Register again refused registration, finding no original authorship in the game. On this issue, the case again worked its way through the district court and then back to Judge Ginsburg, who said that the Copyright Office Register must look at the compilation and not individual parts of the game, stating: "The hallmark of a video game is the expression found in the entire game as it appears and sounds, its sequences of images."[13] With this guidance and clarification, the Copyright Office Register subsequently registered the game, thereby providing Atari with greater protection and enforcement options. Interestingly, this issue—how to classify video games—would arise again in 2011 in the U.S. Supreme Court case *Brown v. Entertainment Merchants, Ass'n*.[14] Once again, the Court compared video games to other types of creative works and again found them protectable, in this case, with First Amendment speech protection.[15] Today, the question is well settled. Video games are protected by copyright so long as they meet the recognized requirements.

Someone's idea for a game is not protected by copyright.[16] Moreover, basic ideas (e.g., a prince runs through a castle to find a princess) are not protected, nor are stock characters. In essence, certain building blocks are available for everyone to use; these elements include noncopyrightable elements already in the public domain, as well as works whose copyright term has expired, putting them likewise in the public domain. Think of Shakespeare's *Romeo and Juliet*,[17] which has been made into *West Side Story*[18] and *Gnomeo and Juliet*.[19] Each uses the story of *Romeo and Juliet* differently as its base, but each is an independent creation. In video games, any number of titles can have teams of players battling each other in an arena, whether it is *Skylanders*,[20] *Defense of the Ancients*,[21] or *League of Legends*.[22] This is called the idea/expression dichotomy, and video game examples of it can be seen in early litigation with Atari.

To gain protection, the game has to be fixed in a tangible medium of expression.[23] This can be a game cartridge, the code itself, or a printed book version of the story, to name three examples. To gain copyright, a video game must also be original—that is, made by a human and independently created. The originality threshold is low—it has to be more than the alphabet—but the idea is that some modicum of creativity must be involved in order to gain protection. In the United States, copyright does not reward "sweat of the brow" labor, only creative labor.[24]

If a work meets the requirements for copyright protection, the copyright holder gains a number of exclusive rights, including the right to reproduce (copy), prepare derivative works, distribute copies, and publicly perform.[25] Infringement occurs when permission was not granted by the copyright holder. There are some exceptions to this, including fair use, which will be discussed in Chapter 4. The basic idea, for now, is that copyright gives the copyright holder certain control in order to license and sell their goods for a set period of time (generally ninety-five years from publication).

In many ways, infringement suits helped define the scope of the video game industry. In the early 1980s, *Pac-Man* was "the most popular video game in the world."[26] When a rival company attempted to release a game called *K.C. Munchkin* that was not identical but resembled the gameplay of *Pac-Man*, the court found copyright infringement where the look and feel of the software was protected by law, writing: "North American [the *K.C. Munchkin* creator] not only adopted the same basic characters but also portrayed them in a manner which made *K.C. Munchkin* appear substantially similar to *Pac-Man*" (618).[27] The court reviewed the two games in much the same way the courts previously had reviewed plays, novels, and films. A year earlier, in 1981, the court in *Atari v. Amusement World*[28] had compared Atari's *Asteroids*[29] to *Meteors*,[30] a potentially infringing game.[31] Unlike the *Pac-Man* knock-off, however, *Meteors* was not found to be infringing because it had only copied the idea, rather than the expression. But both cases signaled that the courts were reviewing video games just as any other copyrightable subject matter.

Another early issue that arose was whether or not players, rather than the game itself, are engaged in "authorship," and in *Midway Mfg. v. Artic International*,[32] the Seventh Circuit found that they are not. At issue was the game *Defender*,[33] and the court analogized the actions of the player as more like changing the channels on a television than creating a derivative work:

> The most he can do is choose one of the limited number of sequences the game allows him to choose. He is unlike a writer or painter because the video game in effect writes the sentences and paints the

painting for him; he merely chooses one of the sentences stored in its memory, one of the paintings stored in its collection.

(pp. 1011–12)

The question of derivative work, whether a player in the act of playing is creating something original, has developed considerably in thirty years. It now widely is acknowledged that players *do* create content (e.g., mods) and interact in much more sophisticated ways with games than in the industry's early days. Still, to this day, the playing of a game itself does not create a derivative work.[34]

Licensed and Unlicensed Works and Hardware[35]

Other legal ambiguities arise when it comes to who is allowed to create games and other hardware for a game system. In many cases, companies may license their intellectual property rights to other parties to create a game for their system. For instance, Nintendo licensed the rights to its *Metroid* franchise to Retro Studios, Inc., for the creation of the 2002 game *Metroid Prime*[36] and its subsequent sequels.

Legal issues arose when unlicensed third parties began developing games for consoles. Between 1983 and 1984, there were a lot of problems in the gaming industry regarding who could create games. In general, anyone with programming knowledge could create and sell games for the Atari 2600 home console. This led to the market being flooded with dozens of inferior-quality games, and as a result, people quickly became wary of purchasing video games. Things changed, however, with the release of the Nintendo Entertainment System and the creation of the "Original Nintendo Seal of Quality" trademark that Nintendo would feature prominently on its products.[37] Nintendo had enough goodwill within the gaming industry that consumers would see the seal of quality and know that it was an officially licensed and endorsed Nintendo product.

Nintendo also developed a "lock-out" method that required a proprietary chip in order to bypass. The lock-out function was called the 10 NES. Officially licensed Nintendo game cartridges contained the chip, and it allowed them to work with the system.

However, the introduction of the "Original Nintendo Seal of Quality" trademark and the 10 NES lock-out method did not stop companies from creating unlicensed games. In the 1980s and 1990s, Color Dreams, Inc., a company that was creating unlicensed games for the Nintendo Entertainment System, managed to reverse-engineer a way to bypass the system's lock-out method and proceeded to create and sell unlicensed games.[38]

Color Dreams eventually dissolved. However, in 1991, they branched off into another company called Wisdom Tree, Inc., that specialized in making Christianity-themed Bible games for home consoles, particularly the Nintendo Entertainment System. Wisdom Tree still exists today, selling many of the same unlicensed games they put out for the Nintendo and Super Nintendo Entertainment Systems. They market their products as "faith oriented video games that target every member of the family."[39] Many of their games are made available through online game download sites such as Steam.[40]

Wisdom Tree's unlicensed Christian game series was brought into the spotlight in 2006 when well-known Internet personality James Rolfe, also known as the "Angry Video Game Nerd" posted his video game review entitled "Bible Games."[41] In the Angry Video Game Nerd series, Rolfe plays a character who uses vulgar language and drinks beer while reviewing games from the 1980s and early 1990s. His main focus is to point out all of the flaws of low-quality games in a humorous fashion. The "Bible Games" video also had two sequels entitled "Bible Games 2" and "Bible Games 3."

Neither Color Dreams' nor Wisdom Tree's games, because they were unlicensed, bore the Nintendo Seal of Quality, and they were obviously low-quality games or blatant rip-offs of other, more successful Nintendo games. One such game was *Spiritual Warfare*[42] for Nintendo Entertainment System. Its start screen displayed a 1992 Wisdom Tree, Inc., copyright. The game involved playing as a Christian man fighting demons and converting non-Christians.[43] However, the game itself was nearly identical to Nintendo's classic game, *The Legend of Zelda*.[44] It used almost identical landscapes, storytelling tactics, and items systems.

Another strange unlicensed game by Wisdom Tree was *Exodus: The Promised Land*. It actually had a message on the front of the cartridge explaining how to play it on the Nintendo Entertainment System, telling the user to turn it on and off at specific intervals, likely to try to bypass the system's lock-out method. One of the more bizarre titles Wisdom Tree created was called *Bible Buffet* in which the player had to fight food monsters and answer Bible questions. Wisdom Tree also put out a game entitled *Super 3D Noah's Ark*. It was the only unlicensed game for the Super Nintendo Entertainment System, but it was not a regular game cartridge. In order to play it, the player had to put it into the cartridge slot and then plug a licensed Nintendo game into the top of it so that it could be read. The game itself was essentially an exact clone of a first-person shooter game called *Wolfenstein 3D*,[45] except instead of playing as a man with a gun shooting Nazis, the player plays as Noah using a slingshot to shoot food at goats and other animals to render them unconscious.[46] Footage of these and other unlicensed games can be found online in the Angry Video Game Nerd's "Bible Games" videos.[47]

Nintendo tolerated both the existence of Color Dreams' and Wisdom Tree's unlicensed games on its game consoles. Likely this was because they wanted to avoid a negative backlash from the general public that might occur if they brought legal suit against a Christian-themed game company.[48] The only officially licensed Christian-themed video game was a 1992 Noah's Ark game created by Konami.[49]

Games were not the only unlicensed forms of hardware for early consoles. In 1990, a company called Lewis Galoob Toys, Inc., created a device called the "Game Genie" for use with the Nintendo Entertainment System. The Game Genie was a device that allowed the user to alter certain aspects of a Nintendo game when used in conjunction with that game. For instance, it could give a player more lives or change the speed at which characters moved. Users could alter up to three codes using the codes provided in the Game Genie manual.[50]

To use a Game Genie, a player would insert it into the game console and then put another game on top of it. It worked "by blocking the value for a single data byte sent by the game cartridge to the central processing unit in the Nintendo Entertainment System and replacing it with a new value."[51] It did not alter the data stored on the game cartridge, and the effects ended when the Game Genie was removed.

Nintendo claimed that the Game Genie was a derivative work and that under 17 U.S.C.A. §106(2), they had the exclusive right to authorize its creation.[52] The appellate court held "[t]he Game Genie merely enhances the audiovisual displays (or underlying data bytes) that originate in Nintendo game cartridges. The altered displays do not incorporate a portion of a copyrighted work in some concrete or permanent form."[53]

Essentially, the court found that the Game Genie did not create a new work in and of itself, but it was merely a way to enhance Nintendo's existing games and enjoy them from a different perspective. They compared use of a Game Genie to play games to the way one might use a kaleidoscope to look at other works of art.

> For example, although there is a market for kaleidoscopes, it does not necessarily follow that kaleidoscopes create unlawful derivative works when pointed at protected artwork. The same can be said of countless other products that enhance, but do not replace, copyrighted works.[54]

Ultimately, the court found that Galoob was not liable under 17 U.S.C. § 107 because the creation of the Game Genie constituted fair use.[55] In response to Nintendo's argument that Galoob was interfering with their right to create and sell their own derivative works, the court stated that "a family's use of a Game Genie for private home enjoyment must be characterized as a non-commercial, nonprofit activity."[56] The court found that Nintendo did not have a basis to claim that the nonprofit, noncommercial uses of the Game Genie harmed them in any way because they had never shown any plans to alter games in the way Game Genie did, nor did there appear to be any kind of market for slightly altered versions of their existing games.[57] In the end, the court allowed Galoob to continue creating Game Genies.

And what about Nintendo video game emulators, the new Game Genies of the twenty-first century? Nintendo explains on its website,

> A Nintendo emulator is a software program that is designed to allow game play on a platform that it was not created for. A Nintendo emulator allows for Nintendo console based or arcade games to be played on unauthorized hardware. The video games are obtained by downloading illegally copied software, i.e. Nintendo ROMs, from Internet distributors. Nintendo ROMs then work with the Nintendo emulator to enable game play on unauthorized hardware such as a personal computer, a modified console, etc.[58]

Nintendo goes on to say:

> The introduction of emulators created to play illegally copied Nintendo software represents the greatest threat to date to the intellectual property rights of video game developers. As is the case with any business or industry, when its products become available for free, the revenue stream supporting that industry is threatened. Such emulators have the potential to significantly damage a worldwide entertainment software industry which generates over $15 billion annually, and tens of thousands of jobs.[59]

Nintendo also sees emulators as hurting their "goodwill," explaining: "The emulator promotes the play of illegal ROMs, NOT authentic games. Thus, not only does it not lead to more sales, it has the opposite effect and purpose."[60]

Today, Nintendo still uses the "Official Nintendo Seal."[61] Nintendo explains, "The official seal is your assurance that this product is licensed by Nintendo. Always look for this seal when buying video game systems, accessories, and related products."[62] On their public website, they explain:

> Below, you will find a list of companies that are licensed to create games, accessories, and other licensed merchandise for Nintendo systems and characters. Use the links below to locate a particular company. If you are unable to find the company you are looking for, please check

to make sure the product you are inquiring about is a **licensed** product. Unlicensed games and accessories are not recommended for use with Nintendo systems.[63]

They list three kinds of licenses: accessory licenses, brand merchandise licenses, and third-party publishers.

Today: Cloned Games[64]

The idea of video game 'cloning' is a particular concern for modern video game developers.[65] 'Clone games' or 'clone-developed games' are games emulated by developers who try to capitalize on the success of the game, or elements of the game, they are copying and use it for their own benefit and profit.[66] Clone developers do not usually copy an entire game but rather copy elements of preexisting games, including original titles, artistic direction, and mechanics.[67]

Software developers, publishers, and video game companies aim to ensure that their games are not copied and used in cloned works.[68] For example, games developed by Sony for their PlayStation console are created on Blu-Ray discs.[69] The ROM-mark serves as a way for these disks to be safeguarded against piracy and mass duplication.[70] More prevalent to the cloning issue is the proliferation of cloned games stemming from mobile gaming platforms, such as the iPhone, Android devices, and tablets, as well as titles released on the three major consoles: PlayStation, Xbox, and Nintendo.[71] Online marketplaces have suffered the most from cloning, with highly successful apps like *Angry Birds*[72] quickly reaching over 100 million downloads on the Apple's App Store.[73] Since then, an abundance of clones have appeared on the App Store, with titles such as *Angry Alien*, *Angry Pig*, *Angry Rhino: RAMPAGE*, and *Angry Animals*.[74] These clones usually are available for free but do have the potential to generate enormous revenue if sold at a price to consumers.[75] An example of costly cloning can be seen in *The Blocks Cometh*, a game created by an independent developer, Halfbot Games.[76] The developers had this game stolen, including the name and art assets, from another developer.[77] The copycat game was released a few days before Halfbot intended to publish its own original work.[78] The cloned game even made it to Apple's top 200 games chart in the App Store and was featured in Apple's New and Noteworthy section, going on to make the top 100 and selling for $0.99.[79]

Two recent cases addressed the question of when a clone version of a game legally infringes. This was a question that had previously been taken up fairly early in litigation. Now, the question arose regarding *Tetris*[80] and a game called *Triple Town*.[81]

Tetris Holding, LLC v. XIO Interactive, LLC is a fairly simple, straightforward case of copyright infringement.[82] Defendant XIO created a Tetris clone called *Mino*.[83] What was interesting was the defense: they argued that they only copied the rules of the game, and rules are not copyrightable—only the expression of the rules. The court did not agree. Some commentators were not happy with how the court approached the idea/expression dichotomy,[84] but the decision also came as a relief to the gaming industry, particularly related to clone games. The worry is that functional elements of a game might be seen as protectable elements, limiting the ability of developers. This was a district court decision, however, and so we will have to wait to see how much impact it actually has. Let's look more carefully at the court's reasoning to provide additional insight into copyright law.

Tetris is known as one of the most famous video games of all time and has been the subject of many cloning attacks since its development in the 1980s.[85] Once the game was exported to the United States, its creator, Alexey Pajitnov, formed Tetris Holding LLC with fellow game designer Henk Rogers.[86] Tetris Holding LLC owned the copyrights to the visual expression of the game.[87] The game has been exported to a number of platforms, including the three main consoles, mobile devices, and computers.[88] Its innovative design revolutionized the puzzle game genre with its unique "falling pieces" that the players could arrange in order to clear lines and earn points.[89] *Tetris* is one of the most popular video games of all time, selling 35 million copies on the Nintendo "Game Boy" alone.[90] In May 2009, Xio Interactive, a video game development company founded by a recent college graduate Desiree Golden, produced *Mino*, a video game strikingly similar to *Tetris*.[91] The physical characteristics of *Mino* mirrored that of *Tetris*, and the game was also distributed via Apple's App Store, giving approximately 6.4 million users access to the game.[92] After numerous takedown notices and the removal of the game from the App Store, *Tetris* brought a suit against Xio for copyright infringement. Xio argued that it only copied uncopyrightable game rules and functionality, rather than a protectable expression.[93] In its analysis, the court described the "general, abstract ideas underlying *Tetris*":

Tetris is a puzzle game where a user manipulates pieces composed of square blocks, each made into a different geometric shape, that fall from the top of the game board to the bottom where the pieces accumulate. The user is given a new piece after the current one reaches the bottom of the available game space. While a piece is falling, the user rotates it in order to fit it in with the accumulated pieces. The object of the puzzle is to fill all spaces along a horizontal line. If that is accomplished, the line is erased, points are earned, and more of the game board is available for play. But if the pieces accumulate and reach the top of the screen, then the game is over.[94]

Some functional aspects of the game, like shadow pieces, garbage lines, and preview pieces, are ideas that inherently facilitate the playing of *Tetris*. Xio used this doctrine as a defense, arguing that the ideas behind the game-play could only be expressed in one way and therefore could not be copyrightable.[95] This is known as the merger doctrine.

The merger doctrine of copyright law states that when there is only one way or a small number of ways to express a particular concept, the expression "merges with the underlying idea"[96] and therefore is unprotectable. The court in *Tetris Holding* stated, "Merger exists when an idea and its particular expression become inseparable."[97] The court concluded that Xio's defense was inapplicable because the court determined there were several possible ways in which Xio could have created its own expression of the rules as set in *Tetris*.[98] Xio's own expert witness unwisely admitted that there could have been an "almost unlimited number" of ways Xio could have designed *Mino* in which the game could have functioned as perfectly as *Tetris* has.[99] The court pointed to the fact that *Tetris* "pieces were not 'necessary to design . . . a puzzle video game.'"[100] It further concluded that because there had been an exponential increase in graphical capabilities over the past two decades, the fact that Xio was unable to design its rules in any other way than those of *Tetris* demonstrated "wholesale copy of its expression."[101] The court concluded that the merger doctrine could not be applied in this instance because there were "many novel ways" in which Xio could have chosen to express and design the rules of the game similar to *Tetris*,[102] but instead they essentially copied the rules and expressed the idea of the game in an almost identical fashion.[103]

The idea–expression dichotomy is one of the fundamental doctrines underlying copyright law and one that served as a focal point in the *Tetris* case. This rule holds that ideas themselves are not the proper subject of copyright protection; only expressions of those ideas are copyrightable.[104] The courts have employed the "abstraction-filtration-comparison" ("AFC") test to determine copyright infringement in video games.[105] The test requires courts to first identify the expanding levels of abstraction in the program.[106] Second, at each level of abstraction, courts must distinguish the material that is protectable by copyright and then filter out the unprotected material for further examination.[107] Essentially, the courts will examine whether there is substantial similarity between the two works, as they have done in the *Tetris* judgment.[108] First the court in the *Tetris* case concluded that the underlying mechanisms and rules of *Tetris* were not protected by copyright.[109] The court held that copyright protects neither the abstract elements of a game nor "the expressive elements that are inseparable from them."[110] Therefore, the basic mechanical components of *Tetris* are void of any protection.[111]

The court did conclude that Tetris Holding was entitled to copyright protection for the way it chose to express its ideas, such as the way it designed the *Tetris* pieces, particularly with respect to the look and feel of the game as presented when the player is viewing and listening to it on the device on which it is being played.[112] Importantly, the court decided to apply a 'layman' test to the case and questioned whether the "gross features of the games" were substantially similar.[113] Placed side by side, the games look almost identical, and so the 'layman' test was easily satisfied.[114] The court further observed that "without being told which is which, a common user would not be able to decipher between the two games."[115] The court reasoned that "if one has to squint to find distinctions only at a granular level, then the works are likely to be substantially similar."[116] The court finally held that the visual similarity between *Tetris* and *Mino* was "akin to literal copying."[117] The obvious similarities of the game visuals, sounds, and mechanics made this case more straightforward than it could have been. Despite not being protected by copyright law, the idea of Xio's game was undoubtedly copied from Tetris, and their expression of that idea was almost identical to the original work.

'Scenes a faire' applies to an expression that is so associated with a particular genre, motif, or idea that one is compelled to use such an expression.[118] Literally it means 'a scene that must be done.' It applies to elements of a work that are stock characters or standard to a particular genre or topic.[119] Over time, these items become traditional aspects of a genre. In the *Tetris* case, Xio wanted the court to apply this doctrine to elements of *Tetris*.[120] If the blocks used in *Tetris*, are "so" associated with a particular idea that one is compelled to use such an expression, there should be no protection under the scenes a faire doctrine.[121] The court in *Tetris Holding* ruled that *Tetris* is a distinct and unique puzzle game that "does not have stock or common imagery that must be included."[122] The court referenced *Incredible Technologies, Inc. v. Virtual Technologies, Inc.*, wherein the court analyzed whether the developer of an arcade golf game infringed on another arcade game because both games employed a trackball that "the user would roll back to simulate a back stroke and then roll forward to simulate the swing itself."[123] The holding of the court is important because it clearly outlines why an element of a game may not be copyrightable. Here, the court asserted that the use of the trackball was functional and not subject to copyright because:

> Like karate, golf is not a game subject to a wholly "fanciful presentation." In presenting a realistic video golf game, one would, by definition, need golf courses, clubs, a selection menu, a golfer, a wind meter, etc. Sand traps and water hazards are a fact of life for golfers, real and virtual. The menu screens are standard to the video arcade game

format, as are the prompts showing the distance remaining to the hole. As such, the video display is afforded protection only from virtually identical copying.[124]

The court in the *Tetris* case reasoned that scenes a faire was inapplicable because *Tetris* is a "wholly fanciful presentation" and a unique puzzle game, and because "it does not have stock or common imagery that must be included."[125] In other words, *Mino* had the option of using other imagery to depict the same idea but ultimately chose to use an almost identical representation. It wasn't necessary for them to use the same imagery because the original *Tetris* game was entirely unique.

The *Spry Fox LLC v. Lolapps, Inc.* decision came out mere days after the *Tetris* decision.[126] The case involved Spry Fox's *Triple Town* and a clone version *Yeti Town*[127] by 6Waves. The clone did not literally copy the original game, but it copied the look and feel. Spry Fox had been in negotiations with Lolapps to make a version for the Apple iOS, but talks had broken down. Once again, the court looked to the idea–expression dichotomy: "The question in this case is not whether the games are similar (they certainly are), but whether that similarity amounts to an infringement of Spry Fox's copyright in Triple Town."[128] As in cases before, the court analyzed the video game in the same way one would review a screenplay: "Spry Fox took the idea underlying Triple Town and expressed it with its own characters, its own setting, and more. These objective elements of expression are within the scope of Spry Fox's copyright."[129] The court found substantial similarity between expressive elements in the cloned game. The court denied the motion to dismiss, and the parties then settled. One commentator wrote: "Game developers should take note: The risks of marketing a clone of another company's innovative video game have risen measurably of late."[130]

Cloning will continue to be a serious concern for game developers aiming to protect their works. The *Tetris Holding* case illustrates the "importance of protecting their work through copyright registration, which is an essential precondition to a lawsuit for copyright infringement."[131] The court's focus on "the overall look and feel of the game"[132] is encouraging for developers because it broadens the potential scope of copyright protection. Improvements in computer processing and graphical capabilities significantly expand the creative limits of game developers. As a result, game developers may have diminishing success in defending a copyright claim against original authors. Moreover, companies like Apple and Samsung should accept more liability for approving games that are blatant copies or clones. If they accept to share in the revenue,[133] they should also accept greater responsibility and provide better safeguards against clones. Without the support of online marketplaces, cloned games would struggle to become popular and reduce potential financial losses by original creators. Other infringements involving the depiction of real-life art in video games will definitely continue to create concerns for developers and the athletes/characters they re-create. As technology progresses, so will the ability of the creator, and audiences will continue to crave a virtual world as close to reality as possible. Copyright laws need to adapt to this changing landscape and make protection for video game developers and artists a priority moving forward.

Notes

1. Alexandra Stork, John Billiris, and Mitchell Longan contributed to writing this chapter.
2. See Chapter 3, Other IP and First Amendment Issues.
3. The World Intellectual Property Organization, WIPO, is a self-funding agency of the United Nations that acts as a global forum for intellectual property development, information, and communication: http://www.wipo.int/about-wipo/en/.
4. Ramos, Andy, Laura Lopez, Anxo Rodriguez, Tim Meng, and Stan Abrams. "The Legal Status of Video Games: Comparative Analysis in National Approaches." *World Intellectual Property Organization.* World Intellectual Property Organization, 2013. Web. 03 Mar. 2016.
5. See Chapter 3, Other IP and First Amendment Issues.
6. "The Legal Status of Video Games" paper goes on to list the creative elements to include: "1. Audio Elements (Musical Compositions, Sound Recordings, Voice, Imported Sound Effects, and Internal Sound Effects), 2. Video Elements (Photographic Images, Digitally Captured Moving Images, Animation, and Text), and 3. Computer Code (Primary Game Engine or Engines, Ancillary Code, Plug-Ins, and Comments). Additionally, other subject matter eligible for copyright protection can include the video game script, its plot and other literary works; well-developed characters; choreographies and pantomimes; and maps and architectural works." Ramos, Andy, Laura Lopez, Anxo Rodriguez, Tim Meng, and Stan Abrams. "The Legal Status of Video Games: Comparative Analysis in National Approaches." *World Intellectual Property Organization.* World Intellectual Property Organization, 2013. Web. 03 Mar. 2016. Section 7.
7. 17.U.S.C. §302. One issue that has arisen is what happens when a game is still under copyright but the company no longer exists or the platform upon which the game is played is no longer maintained or supported.
8. 17 U.S.C. §102(b).
9. Ibid.
10. Atari Games v. Oman. 693 F. Supp 1204. District D.C. 1988.
11. *Breakout*. Atari. Atari, 1976. Arcade game.
12. Atari Games v. Oman. 888 F.2d 878. D.C. Circuit. 1989.
13. Ibid.
14. Brown v. Entertainment Merchants Ass'n. 564 U.S. 1448. Supreme Court 2011.
15. For more on the First Amendment issues, see Chapter 4.
16. They may be protected by contract law, say, if someone agrees to hear ideas and a contract is put in place.

17. Shakespeare, William, and Barbara A. Mowat. *Romeo and Juliet.* New York: Washington Square, 1992. Print.
18. *West Side Story.* Dir. Jerome Robbins and Robert Wise. Perf. Natalie Wood. Comp. Leonard Bernstein. Mirisch Corporation, 1961. Film.
19. *Gnomeo and Juliet.* Dir. Kelly Asbury. Touchstone Pictures, 2011. Film.
20. *Skylanders.* Toys for Bob. Activision, 2011. Multiple platforms.
21. *Defense of the Ancients.* Eul, Steve Feak, and IceFrog, 2003. Mac OS; OS X; Microsoft Windows.
22. *League of Legends.* Riot Games. Riot Games, 2009. Microsoft Windows; OS X. *See also* McArthur, Stephen C. "Clone Wars: The Five Most Important Cases Every Game Developer Should Know." 27 February 2013, http://www. gamasutra.com/view/feature/187385/clone_wars_the_five_most_.php (last visited January 2016).
23. 17 U.S.C. §102(a). Fixation cases related to computers and video games include Stern Electronics v. Kaufman. 2nd Circuit 1982 and Williams Electronics, Inc. v. Arctic International, Inc. 3rd Circuit 1982.
24. For more related to originality in computer and video games, see Atari Games Corp. v. Oman. D.C. Circuit 1989. But in the United Kingdom and other countries, the standards for what counts as labor are different.
25. 17 U.S.C. Section 106: "Subject to sections 107 through 122, the owner of copyright under this title has the exclusive rights to do and to authorize any of the following:

   (1) to reproduce the copyrighted work in copies or phonorecords; (2) to prepare derivative works based upon the copyrighted work; (3) to distribute copies or phonorecords of the copyrighted work to the public by sale or other transfer of ownership, or by rental, lease, or lending; (4) in the case of literary, musical, dramatic, and choreographic works, pantomimes, and motion pictures and other audiovisual works, to perform the copyrighted work publicly; (5) in the case of literary, musical, dramatic, and choreographic works, pantomimes, and pictorial, graphic, or sculptural works, including the individual images of a motion picture or other audiovisual work, to display the copyrighted work publicly; and (6) in the case of sound recordings, to perform the copyrighted work publicly by means of a digital audio transmission."

26. Obias, Rudie. "11 Times Video Games Led to Lawsuits." *Mental Floss.* N.p., 2014. Web. 03 Mar. 2016. http://mentalfloss.com/article/55078/11-times-video-games-led-lawsuits
27. Atari v. North American. 672 F. 2d 607 Supreme Court 1982.
28. Atari v. Amusement World. 547 F. Supp. 222. Supreme Court 1981.
29. *Asteroids.* Atari. Atari, 1979. Arcade game.
30. *Meteors.* Amusement World. Amusement World, 1980. Coin-operated.
31. Ian Bogost, Meteors: An Obscure Title at the center of videogame copyright litigation is unearthed 30 years later, http://bogost.com/writing/blog/meteors/
32. Midway Mfg. v. Artic International. 704 F.2d 1009. Supreme Court 1983.
33. *Defender.* Williams Electronics. Williams Electronics, 1981. Arcade game.
34. Other historical cases include: Atari v. Amusement World Inc. District Court of Maryland. November 1981; Data East USA, Inc. v. Epyx, Inc. 9th Circuit 1988; Capcom U.S.A. Inc. v. Data East Corp. Northern District of California 1994; Ringgold v. Black Entertainment Television, Inc. Second Circuit 1997; Cavalier v. Random House, Inc. Ninth Circuit 2002; and Lewis Galloob Toys, Inc. v. Nintendo of America. Ninth Circuit 1992.

35. This section is written by Alexandra Stork.
36. *Metroid Prime*. Retro Studios. Nintendo, 2002. Game Cube; Wii.
37. Arnone, John M. "Game (Not) Over: How a Mark Saved Video Games." *Journal of Contemporary Legal Issues* 19. 247 (2010). http://connection.ebscohost.com/c/articles/52365326/game-not-over-how-mark-saved-video-games.
38. "Color Dreams, Inc." *Giant Bomb*. CBS Interactive, Inc., n.d. Web. 03 Mar. 2016.
39. "Who Is Wisdom Tree, Inc." *About Wisdom Tree*. Wisdom Tree, Inc., 2015–16. Web. 03 Mar. 2016.
40. "Wolfenstein 3D PC Game." *Steam*. Valve Corporation, 2016. Web. 03 Mar. 2016.
41. Matei, Mike. "AVGN: Bible Games." *Cinemassacre*. Cinemassacre Productions, LLC, 2013. Web. 03 Mar. 2016.
42. "Spiritual Warfare." *Giant Bomb*. CBS Interactive, Inc., 2016. Web. 03 Mar. 2016.
43. Ibid.
44. *The Legend of Zelda*. Nintendo. Nintendo, 1986. Nintendo Entertainment System.
45. *Wolfenstein 3D*. id Software. Apogee, 1992. MS-DOS.
46. "Super Noah's Ark 3D." *Super Noah's Ark 3D (Game)*. CBS Interactive, Inc., 2016. Web. 03 Mar. 2016.
47. Matei, Mike. "AVGN: Bible Games." *Cinemassacre*. Cinemassacre Productions, LLC, 25 December 2006. Web. 03 Mar. 2016; Matei, Mike. "AVGN: Bible Games 2." *Cinemassacre*. Cinemassacre Productions, LLC, 23 December 2008. Web. 03 Mar. 2016; Matei, Mike. "AVGN: Bible Games 3." *Cinemassacre*. Cinemassacre Productions, LLC, 07 December 2011. Web. 03 Mar. 2016.
48. Arnone, John M. "Game (Not) Over: How a Mark Saved Video Games." *Journal of Contemporary Legal Issues* 19. 247 (2010). http://connection.ebscohost.com/c/articles/52365326/game-not-over-how-mark-saved-video-games.
49. "Noah's Ark NES." *MobyGames*. Blue Flame Labs, 17 November 2007. Web. 03 Mar. 2016. http://www.mobygames.com/game/noahs-ark
50. Lewis Galoob Toys, Inc. v. Nintendo of America, Inc. 964 F.2d 965. 9th Circuit 1992 at 967.
51. Ibid.
52. 17 U.S.C.A. §106(2).
53. Lewis Galoob Toys, Inc. v. Nintendo of America, Inc. 964 F.2d 965. 9th Circuit 1992.
54. Ibid.
55. 17 U.S.C.A. § 107.
56. Lewis Galoob Toys, Inc. v. Nintendo of America, Inc. 964 F.2d 965. 9th Circuit 1992.
57. Ibid.
58. Nintendo, Legal Information (Copyrights, Emulators, ROMs, etc.), https://www.nintendo.com/corp/legal.jsp.
59. Ibid.
60. Ibid.
61. "Character Merchandise, Gaming Accessories and Third Party Publishers." *Nintendo*, https://www.nintendo.com/corp/licensees.jsp.
62. "Licensed and Unlicensed Products." *Nintendo*, https://www.nintendo.com/consumer/licensed.jsp.
63. Ibid.

64. This section is written by John Brilliris.
65. Schecter, Jack. "Grand Theft Video: Judge Gives Gamemakers Hope for Combating Clones." *Susteinlaw.com*. Sustein Kann Murphy & Timbers LLP, June 2012. Web. 2012, http:/susteinlaw.com/grand-theft—video-judge-gives-gamemakers-hope-for-combating-clones/
66. Ibid.
67. Ibid.
68. Pflake, James. "Why SimCity's DRM Is a Necessary Evil." *ExtremeTech*. Extreme Tech, 07 March 2013. Web. 07 Mar. 2013, http://www.extremetech.com/gaming/150240-why-simscity-drm-is-a-necessary-evil e a user manipulates pieces com[layed on consoles or machines in aracde over-app-store-fees-report/. blatant copies or clones. I.
69. Sony. "Play Station 4 User's Guide." *Manuals Play Station*. N.p., n.d. Web. 2016, http://manuals.playstation.net/document/en/ps4/videos/videodisc.html.
70. Ibid.
71. Curtis, Tom. "Apple Removes Several IOS Copycat Games from One Offending Developer." *Gamasutra Article*. Gamasutra, n.d. Web. 03 Feb. 2016, www.gamasutra.com/view/news/40101/Apple_removes_several_iOS_copycat_games_from_one_offending_developer.php.
72. *Angry Birds*. Rovio Mobile. Chillingo/Clickgamer, 2009. iOS.
73. Haas, Pete. "Angry Birds Hits 100 Million Downloads." *Cinema Blend*. Cinema Blend, n.d. Web. 2012, http://www.cinemablend.com/games/Angry-Birds-Hits-100-Millions-Downloads-30659.html.
74. Meyers, Justin. "Angry Clones Are Taking Over the App Store." *Business Insider*. Business Insider, n.d. Web. 03 May 2011, http://articles.businessinsider.com/2011–05–03/tech/29954973_1_rovio-mobile-devices-windows-phone e a user manipulates pieces com[layed on consoles or machines in aracde over-app-store-fees-report/. blatant copies or clones. I.
75. Ibid.
76. Webster, Andrew. *The Clones Cometh: The App Store Is Full of Copycats, and It's Indies Who Suffer*, Ars Technica, February, http://arstechnica.com/gaming/2011/02/halfbot-interview/
77. Ibid.
78. Ibid.
79. Ibid.
80. *Tetris*. AcademySoft/Spectrum Holobyte. AcademySoft/Spectrum Holobyte/Tandy, 1984. Multiple platforms.
81. *Triple Town*. Spry Fox, 2010. Multiple platforms.
82. Tetris Holding, LLC v. XIO Interactive, LLC. 863 F. Supp. 2d 394. District New Jersey 2012.
83. *Mino*. Xio, 2009, http://ipspotlight.com/2012/06/12/looks-like-tetris-video-game-clones-and-copyright-law/
84. See Sam Castree II, "A Problem Old as Pong: Video Game Cloning and the Proper Bounds of Video Game Copyrights." http://papers.ssrn.com/sol3/papers.cfm?abstract_id=2322574.
85. *Bios*, Tetris, http://www.tetris.com/about-tetris/bio/alexey-pajitnov.aspx (last visited April 21, 2013).
86. "Tetris", *Wikipedia*. Wikimedia Foundation, n.d. Web. 05 Mar. 2016, https://en.wikipedia.org/wiki/Tetris (last visited February 26, 2016).
87. Ibid.

88. Ibid.
89. Ibid.
90. Ibid.
91. Tetris Holding at 397.
92. See, "iPhone Users Watch More Video . . . and Are Older Than You Think."
    Nielsen Wire, 10 June 2009, http://www.nielsen.com/us/en/newswire/2009/
    iphone-users-watch-more—video-and-are-older-than-you-think.html
93. Tetris Holding at 411.
94. Ibid. at 409.
95. Ibid.
96. Capcom U.S.A., Inc. v. Data East Corp. Northern District Cal. 1994 at 26.
97. Tetris Holding at 403 (citing Kay Berry, Inc. v. Taylor Gifts, Inc. 421 F.3d 199,
    209. 3rd Circuit 2005).
98. Ibid.
99. Ibid. at 412.
100. Ibid.
101. Ibid.
102. Ibid.
103. Ibid.
104. See 17 U.S.C. § 102.
105. Atari Inc. v. N. AM. Philips Consumer Elects' Corp. 672 F.2d 607. 7th Circuit
    1982 and MIdway Mfg. Co. v. Bandai-Am. Inc. 546 F. Supp. 125. District
    Court N.J. 1982.
106. Ibid.
107. Ibid. at 707.
108. Tetris Holding at 412.
109. Ibid. at 404.
110. Ibid. at 409.
111. Ibid.
112. Ibid. at 404.
113. Ibid. at 409 (citing Universal Athletic Sales Co. v. Stalked. 511 F.2d 904. 908.
    3rd Circuit 1975. Print.).
114. Ibid.
115. Ibid. at 410.
116. Ibid.
117. Ibid.
118. Ibid. at 412.
119. Ibid.
120. Ibid.
121. Ibid. at 403–8.
122. Ibid. at 412.
123. Ibid. at 408; See also Incredible Techs. Inc. v. Virtual Techs. Inc. 400 F.3d
    1007. 7th Circuit 2005. Print.
124. Ibid.
125. Ibid. at 412.
126. Spry Fox LLC v. Lolapps, Inc. 2012 Westlaw 5290158. Western District Wash
    2012.
127. *Yeti Town.* 6Waves. 2011. iOS.
128. Spry Fox LLC v. Lolapps, Inc. 2012 Westlaw 5290158. Western District Wash 2012.
129. Ibid.

130. Schecter, Jack. "Bears Beat Yetis! Another Copyright Defeat for Video Game Clones." *Sunstein*. N.p., October 2012. Web. Jan. 2016, http://sunsteinlaw. com/bears-beat-yetis-another-copyright-defeat-for-video-game-clones/.
131. Schecter, Jack. "Grand Theft Video: Judge Gives Gamemakers Hope for Combating Clones." *Sunstein*. N.p., June 2012. Web, http://sunsteinlaw.com/ grand-theft-video-judge-gives-gamemakers-hope-for-combating-clones/ (See citation 36, in email from Oscar).
132. Tetris Holding at 409.
133. Reisinger, Don. "Microsoft, Apple in Battle Over App Store Fees—Report." *CNET*. N.p., Dec. 2012. Web, http://new.cnet.com/8301–13579_3–57558482–37/ microsoft-apple-in-battle-over-app-store-fees-report.

3 Legal Issues Beyond Copyright[1]

Although copyright is the traditional mechanism to protect the video game itself—the story, plot, graphics, and characters—trademark runs a close second in importance, as the brands of both the video game itself and the company producing them grew in stature. Think of *World of Warcraft*, *Pokémon*, or *Skylanders*. All three are global brands, and it is through licensing of both the copyright and the trademark that their revenue grows.

Trademarks

Trademark is the second major legal apparatus that can protect a number of video game elements, especially its brand. Trademarks are usually registered with the U.S. Patent and Trademark Office and provide protection from other "brands" trying to use similar marks that would cause consumer confusion. Famous brands are provided even greater protection from "dilution." Dilution comes in two forms: tarnishment (e.g., *Debbie Does Dallas*,[2] a pornographic film using Dallas Cowboy cheerleading costumes) and blurring (e.g., Federal Espresso, a coffee house using a name similar to and invoking Federal Express, the overnight delivery company). The idea is that very famous marks have built up their reputations and others should not be able to ride the coattails of that work.[3] Brand protection for the video game industry is important, particularly as the industry has expanded into merchandising and other tie-ins related to the main video game.

Don McGowan, general counsel of *Pokémon* and formerly of the Game Division of Microsoft, framed the issue of legal protection as inbound (defending the brand) and outbound (commercializing the brand). *Pokémon* as a media franchise includes video games, toys, and merchandising, as well as a production company, to name just some of its many aspects. *Pokémon* is usually one of the top three in brand value each year, and as general counsel, McGowan's job is to legally manage the interplay between protection and promotion.

In 2008, in *E.S.S. Entertainment 2000, Inc. v. Rock Star Videos, Inc.*, the Ninth Circuit Appeals Court ruled in favor of the video game developer Rock Star in a dispute involving trade dress and trademark infringement, citing First Amendment protection.[4] The case involved a real-life strip club, called the Play Pen's Gentlemen Club, being represented in the video game *Grand Theft Auto*[5] as a club called the Pig's Pen.[6] In the game, the logo for the fictional club is inspired by and uses elements of the real-life Play Pen's trademarked logo.[7] The court ruled that there was no nominative use, as the map designer intended for the Pig's Pen logo to evoke the image of the Play Pen and there was no real comment or criticism on the Play Pen itself.[8] However, the court went on to say that the use of the Pig's Pen imagery was consistent with the theme of the game, namely a cartoony reimagining of Los Angeles.[9] The only way a use of trademark would not be protected in the court's eyes was if it had "no artistic relevance to the underlying work whatsoever. In other words, the level of artistic relevance must be above zero."[10] Furthermore, the court contended that there was no reasonable way for an individual to have brand confusion when it came to the name Pig's Pen and the similar trade dress because it would be far-fetched for an individual to believe that the game was produced by the strip club or that the video game company owns a strip club.[11]

Thus, First Amendment use of trademarks seems to be pretty well protected when it comes to video games. Brand confusion arguments are difficult to make because a video game usually does not compete with the direct market of the brand itself. The Ninth Circuit is a leader in setting the First Amendment threshold for protection (most likely because many video game companies are within the Ninth Circuit region) and they have set the threshold very low.

Another case to look at involves Mil-Spec-Monkey (MSM) suing Activision Blizzard for the use of their mark in the *Call of Duty* franchise. This is a more blatant example of use of trademark because the mark was used unaltered, compared to the *Grand Theft Auto* case.[12] The court, however, still ruled in the favor of Activision Blizzard.[13] In the game *Call of Duty Ghosts*[14] the player is able to customize their player with icons selected from the game. One of the icons is an unaltered trademarked MSM logo. Using the standard set in the *Grand Theft Auto* case, they ruled that its artistic relevance was at least greater than zero, due to the fact that *Call of Duty Ghosts* was a military-themed game and MSM produces military products.[15] The court also found that the use of the logo was not misleading and that Activision Blizzard did not make any explicit effort to suggest a relationship between the two companies.[16] Given this, it would suggest that the Ninth Circuit has offered great protection to the use of trademarks within video games.

Patents[17]

Patents are exclusive proprietary rights granted by the government to the owner of a claimed invention.[18] Generally, the use of patents to protect innovation attempts to strike a careful balance between exclusive rights that incent invention and the chilling effect that results from prohibiting unauthorized use.[19] In the video game industry, a wide variety of inventions and features are eligible for patent protection, some more obviously within the scope of patent law than others.

Patents are enormously valuable in the video game industry. The ability to exclude the competition allows a patent holder to stay dominant in a gaming genre by keeping others from the breakthrough ideas that drive commercial appeal.[20] Moreover, a patent prevents reverse engineering, unlike protections in copyright law. As a result, royalties in video games can be extremely profitable for successful inventions as the only means to utilize patented innovations.[21] The revenues secured through patent protections increase research and development budgets and can inspire creative works.[22]

However, as mentioned, patent protections can also cause a chilling effect on the video game industry. Fear of infringing patented hardware and software can limit innovation and investment efforts. Patent litigation can result in multimillion-dollar claims, royalties, injunctions, or scrapped projects. Particularly litigious patent holders can drive opponents from competition with the threat of legal action alone. Further, a patent holder need not be exclusively in the video game industry to defend their patents against use in video game technology.

For example, Nintendo recently won an appeal over a Wii controller that allegedly utilized the same technology as a patented pointer designed for office presentations.[23] The case turned on whether the patent was for a direct or indirect pointing system, with the court ultimately deciding that the references to indirect pointing inferiority limited the claim to only direct pointing technology. Nintendo escaped liability, but the action proved yet again that the threat of patent infringement across a variety of fields is a very real concern for the industry as it evolves.

Key Differences Between Copyright and Patent Protections in Video Games

The Patent Office grants patents for gaming system features, accessories, controllers, and other hardware improvements, but also for certain visual-intensive methods and elements of gameplay.[24] As a result, legal issues can overlap, and video game developers will often hold both a patent and a copyright in their works, and patent holders will often sue for copyright and patent infringement in the same actions. Nintendo, for example, maintains copyrights in software source code, executable code, game visual display, game music, game characters, product packaging, game manuals, labels, hardware chip microcode, artwork, and publications. Additionally, they hold "many utility and design patents associated with Nintendo's hardware and software products," as well as trademarks in gaming systems and franchises.[25]

A major difference between copyrights and patents, for the most part, is that copyright law does not protect against reverse engineering. Copyright law specifically outlines reverse engineering as a legal §1201 circumvention of copyright protection systems in many circumstances.[26] Where reverse engineering is the only way to gain access to the ideas and functional elements embodied in a copyrighted computer program and where there is a legitimate reason for seeking such access, reverse engineering is a fair use of the copyrighted work.[27] For example, when Nintendo pioneered the NES10 lockout system preventing unauthorized video game development to maximize license revenues, Atari simply reverse engineered the source code. Though the trial court disagreed, the court of appeals stated that reverse engineering would not constitute copyright infringement and could be a fair use, provided that the product was rightfully possessed.[28]

Patent law does not concern itself with the means of infringement and protects against stealing the benefit of a patented invention by only changing "minor or insubstantial details of the claimed invention while retaining the same functionality."[29] The essential inquiry into patent infringement is simply "whether the accused product contains elements identical or equivalent to each claimed element of the patented invention."[30]

The Scope of Patents in Video Games

Not surprisingly, hardware and accessories comprise a large portion of video game patents. One of the most successful patents was Nintendo's D-Pad, a controller feature for multidirectional movement in two-dimensional worlds.[31] The patent on the simple "plus sign" directional pad design for movement up, down, left, and right allowed Nintendo to exclude others from utilizing similar D-Pad controllers until it expired in 2005.[32] The patent was a tremendous obstacle for other control designers, such as Xbox, who could not solve their directional pad problems without infringing on the D-Pad patent.[33] Other controller-related patents include wireless technology, vibrations, motion sensors, and the specific controller designs that accompany each new system release.

Game consoles also patent new features with each release. Xbox patented online game invitations and a system of completing "achievements" and receiving awards.[34] As a result, a few years after Xbox could not produce a functional directional pad, Nintendo could not invite friends to play online without typing out "Friend Codes."[35] Looking forward, it appears Xbox has a patent for DVR recording, which suggests their next release could integrate DVR features directly into the console interface.[36]

Copyright law is not, however, the only protection afforded to the look and feel of a video game. The technology-intensive elements of video games render some visual elements in gameplay eligible for both patent and copyright protection. In video games, a patent covers "software like game-play techniques, score-calculation methods and graphics engineers" and "hardware like elements of a console or its accessories."[37] The result is a wide range of patents that cover nearly every element of the industry. In fact, patents protect gameplay elements such as giving on-screen directions, battle methods, methods of engaging enemies, and even a method of penalizing gamers who break rules in video games.[38] The wide scope of software protections afforded through patent law has shaped the industry.

The widespread applicability of patents in video games and the nature of video game development mean that hardware manufacturers and software publishers alike both invest in research and development for patentable innovation. As a result, leading publishers have a handful of interesting patents. For example, Electronic Arts holds patents for key features in gameplay from highly successful sports franchises and a few avatar-related patents from *The Sims*.[39] Surprisingly, they also have patents on saving game data in cross-platform cloud hard drives and a console with a wireless controller.[40] Activision has a patent on social networking integration in video game consoles.[41]

Smaller publishers have invested heavily in patents as well and control a disproportionate number of patents for their market share. Though not nearly as recognizable as Electronic Arts or Activision, Square Enix and Konami dominate the field. Square Enix has patents in video games with fast-forward and slow-motion features, penalties for players that violate game rules, and network connectivity upgrades, in addition to 139 other patents.[42] Konami Digital Entertainment holds 257 patents, including a device that deciphers musical genres.[43]

With such wide applicability and high returns on successful patents, the video game industry is filled with a variety of highly invested players. Because everything from gameplay innovation to hardware upgrades can be patented, patent litigation shaped video game development since *Pong*[44] was released in 1972.

Patent Litigation in Video Games

The first video game patent was for a "television gaming apparatus" that used a paddle-type control to move onscreen objects that collided with other onscreen objects. The patent was licensed to Magnavox, who created the first *Pong* game and the first video game console, launching a multibillion-dollar industry.

In the first major legal action regarding the *Pong* patent, Magnavox sued Atari for copying their highly successful game. In 1976, Atari settled out of court and paid licensing and royalty fees to Magnavox while continuing to sell *Pong* games.[45] Ultimately, litigation proved highly successful for Magnavox, as the company successfully defended their patent against wave after wave of infringement issues over the next decade. Litigation involved console hardware, paddle controllers, and software issues relating to *Pong* gameplay. The successful actions across such varying elements of video game development proved that a strong patent is the perfect way to protect intellectual property.[46]

Magnavox was far from the only company involved in hardware litigation relating to patents. A decade later, Atari was involved in litigation with Nintendo, which had emerged as the leading game console of the 1980s. In an attempt to circumvent the licensing process that Nintendo used for video game developers, Atari unlocked the NES10 authorization software through reverse engineering. Nintendo sued, and the case settled out of court. In 1996, Nintendo would again be involved in litigation regarding its console hardware when Alpex Computer Corp. sued for a graphics technique used in the NES.[47] After the trial court awarded Alpex more than 250 million dollars in damages, the appellate court found that Nintendo's innovative shift-register approach to graphics was not covered by a narrow interpretation of the patent at issue.[48] The graphics system would pave the way for modern video games, but was nearly derailed by the tremendous trial court judgment.

In another example of the key differences between patent and copyright litigation in video games, Sega lost a lawsuit over the reverse engineering of the Genesis console. After Accolade failed to agree to production terms, the company simply determined the requirements of the Genesis system. Because Sega had failed to acquire a patent on Sega Genesis, the court ruled against Sega. Sega lost the ability to license video game manufacturing rights, and the system soon became obsolete.

Patents for video game hardware go well beyond console issues. Another crucial component of innovative video game manufacturing lies in the controller, where a critical balance of sophistication and comfort is built into new designs. Recently, Nintendo won a case brought by UltimatePointer regarding a direct-pointing system for office presentations. The court recognized that Nintendo used an indirect pointing system and held that because the UltimatePointer patent criticized indirect pointing technology, the claims only applied to direct pointing technology.[49] The case demonstrated an attack from another industry on the profitability of video game manufacturing.

Another key battleground with controllers was over vibration features. Whereas consoles like Nintendo 64 and Sega Dreamcast utilized inserts to create a vibrating sensation, Sony integrated vibration directly into the controller. The vibration technology infringed on an Immersion patent, and video game giant Sony was forced to pay more than 90 million dollars in damages while suffering a permanent injunction. Wireless controller features have been similarly contested as the technology continues to be widely used and improved upon.

Software patent litigation is also commonplace. Whether gameplay too closely mirrors a patented element of a game already on the market or a patented feature merely excludes others from creating a similar game, the design patents awarded to visual software innovation have a tremendous impact on the market. Because of the sweeping patents that issue for gameplay features and visual methods, potential areas of infringement can significantly limit developers.

Recently, a fantasy sports software company sued Activision, claiming the real-time interaction systems utilized in Activision games infringed on fantasy sports patents. Where fantasy sports interfaces must collect real-time statistics to tally scores, sports video games can also aggregate statistics in real time to make competition more exciting.[50] Again, although Activision does not appear to be involved in fantasy sports, an outside industry attacked a successful video game producer. With fantasy sports now a 27-billion-dollar industry, the patents at issue were also licensed to producers like Electronic Arts, Konami, and even Microsoft for video game development.[51]

As demonstrated by Alpex's lawsuit against Nintendo, when a trial court can erroneously find that the next big breakthrough in video game graphics technology is a 250-million-dollar infringement of dated technology, the perils of patent litigation become obvious. Video game developers must constantly balance potential catastrophic infringement issues with the benefits of winning the next big console war or producing a revolutionary video game.

That said, when a major console manufacturer neglects to patent their invention, the necessity of intellectual property protections becomes equally clear. The right of an inventor to demand a profit for an innovative breakthrough must be protected. Licensing and royalty arrangements allow for a risk–reward paradigm that leads to more innovation without necessarily curtailing creativity in the current market.

For now, the risk seems worth the reward as billion-dollar companies rise and fall with technological breakthroughs. Expansive patent protections that span software and hardware innovation appear to strike the appropriate balance between encouraging creativity and protecting inventors. Licensing and royalty rights appear to be liberally distributed to video game developers, lest a hardware manufacturer miss out on a game that could irreparably benefit a rival console.

Because of the intense competition between battling brands at every level of the video game industry, the current patent scheme maximizes creative incentive. Competing consoles want the best games to be compatible with their new systems, while constantly incorporating new features and better graphics in an effort to get ahead. Video game producers gain little from copying the successful features of other games because novel gameplay drives sales. When competition fails to maintain stability, parties can always fall back on multimillion-dollar litigation to secure interests. Right now in the video game industry, it seems everyone benefits from abundant patents with liberal licensing agendas.

Contract Issues

Video games have also inspired cases related to end user license agreements (EULAs), terms of use, and terms of service. Issues arise relating to the enforceability of such contracts,[52] what constitutes the public performance of video games,[53] and in-game advertising.[54] We also see contract questions and other legal issues arise in virtual worlds, which are governed by terms of service and use. The question is this: What happens when the issues arising go beyond the contract to, say, criminal activity? What is the difference between a virtual crime and an actual crime?

One of the most famous cases regarding terms of use and end user license agreements is the 2010 Ninth Circuit decision in *MDY Industries, LLC. v. Blizzard Entertainment and Vivendi Games, Inc.*[55] The case concerned *World of Warcraft* (*WoW*), a multiplayer online game with seventy levels. Michael Donnelly developed and sold *Glider*,[56] a software program that automatically played the beginning levels of *WoW* for players. Donnelly sought a declaratory judgment that his program did not infringe any *WoW* copyrights. The district court found secondary copyright infringement and violation of Section 1201 of the Copyright Act.

The court of appeals took up the questions again. First, the court found that *WoW* players do not own copies of the software, but are licensees, where Blizzard reserves the right to impose restrictions, and may not sell or give away the account. As part of the EULA, players are restricted from using unauthorized third-party programs, and Blizzard may terminate user accounts if players violate the terms of use or the EULA. If the usage is not within the scope of Blizzard's limited license, the use would be infringing.

The court also distinguished between a contractual covenant and a license condition. Contract terms that limit a license's scope are "conditions," and the court explains, "the break of which constitute copyright infringement." In contrast, a "covenant" is a breach, which is actionable only under contract law. The court found that under the terms of use, the prohibition against bots and unauthorized third-party software comprised contractual covenants: "Here, *WoW* players did not commit copyright infringement by using *Glider* in violation of the ToU [terms of use]. MDY is thus not liable for secondary copyright infringement, which requires the existence of direct copyright infringement."[57]

Right of Publicity[58]

What Is Right of Publicity?

Celebrities and even private individuals (in some states) have the right to control the commercial use of their likeness. Video games often license with celebrities to use their images, voice, and story. Right of publicity prevents the unauthorized commercial use of an individual's name, likeness, or other recognizable aspects of one's persona.[59] Where recognized, the law has roots in state common law or is explicitly granted by statute.[60] Many right-of-publicity protections are outlined through state right-of-privacy laws, which prevent intrusion, appropriation of name or likeness, unreasonable publicity, and portrayal in a false light.[61] Nearly half of the states, however, do not have explicit right-of-publicity protections and rely instead on unfair competition, misappropriation, and trademark law.[62]

The Restatement (Third) of Unfair Competition specifically outlines liability under right of publicity, declaring that "one who appropriates the commercial value of a person's identity by using without consent the person's name, likeness, or other indicia of identity for purposes of trade is subject to liability."[63] By law, right-of-publicity protections extend to every individual. Because right of publicity centers on commercial use, however, disputes typically involve celebrities and individuals with highly recognizable names and likenesses.[64] Now that gaming systems are more capable of realistically portraying individuals, the issue is a more relevant consideration for the industry before launching a project.

Right of publicity must reconcile individual rights with First Amendment creative expression and protections for appropriation used for public

entertainment purposes.[65] Despite more than fifty years of acceptance and
case law, the judiciary has struggled with right-of-publicity cases where
First Amendment expression is involved.[66] Four tests have emerged as
standards used by divided state courts that lack substantive guidance.[67]
Those tests include the "actual malice" test,[68] "transformative" test,[69] "artistic relevance" test,[70] and "predominant purpose" test.[71]

The inconsistency in state court analyses complicates right-of-publicity
claims overall, and varying tests could resolve similar claims in different
ways. As defenses arise from case-by-case circumstances, a clear standard
cannot be delineated. Generally, the judiciary lacks a consistent and princi-
pled approach to resolving First Amendment issues with right-of-publicity
claims.[72] Scholars call for clarity, flexibility, and modification of existing
approaches.[73] When applied to video games and its wildly evolving capabilities, right-of-publicity litigation remains relatively open-ended.

Despite the significant limitations of eight-bit graphics technology, early
video games often required licensing. Games such as *Death Race*,[74] *Tron*,[75]
and *Raiders of the Lost Ark*[76] recognized that basing video games on identi-
fiable movies could improve commercial viability.[77] In 1982, *Raiders of the
Lost Ark* on Atari 2600 became the first ever movie-licensed video game.[78]
Later that year, the first-ever officially licensed *Star Wars*[79] game was also
released.[80] The Atari licenses proved that as early as the 1970s and 1980s,
video games, in proper context, could accurately portray real-life characters
for commercial gain.

Eventually, three-dimensional game worlds and expanded storylines
became a major focus of the video game industry and a key feature in
new gaming systems. PlayStation and Nintendo 64 rendered older gaming
platforms obsolete with tremendous graphics improvements.[81] Franchises
began to focus more on one main character with a recognizable persona as
character development capabilities improved.

Early right-of-publicity claims in video games were based more on name
and context. Mistaken admissions of guilt relating to the inspiration behind
the characters often were decisive in early court decisions.[82] As the video
game industry developed and more specific details were incorporated into
characters, right-of-publicity actions also evolved. Courts were forced to
evaluate sophisticated designs with expressive elements against the recognizable images and personas they may call to mind.

Because right-of-publicity laws are entirely rooted in state law and there
is no sweeping legislation for courts to turn to, inconsistent case law prece-
dents and nuanced decisions lay conflicting groundwork to evaluate present
issues.[83] Multiple tests are applied to video game right-of-publicity cases in
an effort to find a case-by-case balance between First Amendment protected
expression and the private rights of individuals to their own image. As a

result, the full extent of right-of-publicity claims in video games, which are afforded the same expressive protections as books and movies, will often vary considerably by jurisdiction.[84]

Right of Publicity in Sports Video Games

Sports video games are outrageously successful. Industry leader EA Sports eclipsed 4 billion dollars in annual sales revenue and continues to grow.[85] Goals for EA Sports add-on content alone exceeded 1 billion dollars in the 2015 fiscal year, with a new video game released at the beginning of each season.[86] Sports video games give players an opportunity to manage every aspect of their favorite sports franchise, take a player through a professional sports career, or play competitively online.

Given the popularity of sports video games and professional athletes, the industry would appear to be ripe with right-of-publicity legal issues. Athletes are icons, and the right to capitalize on sports fame is protected by state law right of publicity. Typically, however, all players must join a players' union that contracts away many right-of-publicity claims that would be commercially useful in video games.[87] Most professional sports leagues use a licensing system for third-party content featuring groups of athletes, such as the rosters in sport video games.[88] Though such licenses do not typically govern the use of a single athlete, the league licenses the rights to the entire player universe as a whole.[89]

Licenses have been a profitable instrument for professional sports leagues, but also allow video game developers to gain exclusive production rights as the only official video game of a sport.[90] For example, for its 2K Sports franchise, *MLB: The Show*,[91] Take Two Interactive was able to obtain an exclusive Major League Baseball license and corner the market.[92] Despite EA Sports at the time having the more successful *MVP Baseball*[93] franchise, the seven-year license obtained by Take Two Interactive drove EA Sports out of Major League Baseball video games.[94] Take Two Interactive's 2K Sports franchise quickly became the only baseball game on the market because EA Sports could not produce a viable baseball game without any player rights. The licensing maneuver came shortly after EA Sports acquired an exclusive NFL license of their own for its *Madden*[95] franchise.[96]

Licensing proves the value of right of publicity of athletes. In one of the first right-of-publicity cases in video games relating to sports, Todd McFarlane created a villainous character named Antonio "Tony Twist" Twistelli in his *Spawn* comic book and video game series.[97] McFarlane later admitted to using the name of St. Louis Blues hockey player, Anthony Twistelli, as the basis for the character's name in a magazine article.[98] The Missouri court awarded Twistelli 15 million dollars in damages based on the appropriation of his name, based largely on the admission by McFarlane that he named his character after the hockey player.[99] The court found that the use of the NHL player's name was not protected speech under the First Amendment despite the character having little resemblance to Anthony Twistelli.[100] The court weighed the admission heavily against McFarlane, and it may have been a decisive factor.

In another series of cases that ultimately drove EA Sports from video games based on college sports, college football and basketball players sued EA Sports for the use of their likenesses. The licensing system of professional sports did not exist to consolidate player rights at the college level, as the athletes in the actions were not paid, did not join a union, and did not otherwise concede their individual player rights. As a result, EA Sports attempted to create a college football game without the permission of the individual players involved by using only player numbers without player names while operating under a license agreement with the NCAA for team logos and other marks.[101]

Quarterback Ryan Hart led a suit against EA Sports in the Third Circuit, claiming the video game series had appropriated his likeness. Sam Keller led another lawsuit in the Ninth Circuit. Ultimately, Keller's case settled for 40 million dollars and included Ryan Hart.[102] The decisive Keller case turned on the determination that the use of player likenesses was not sufficiently transformative to warrant First Amendment protection.[103] Surprisingly, however, the courts were not uniform in this adoption of the transformative use test.[104] The Third Circuit found that video games are interactive in nature and that even untransformed images of Hart were transformative if the option to edit was included in the gameplay.[105] Hart would have received no award in the Third Circuit if that decision held up. The Ninth Circuit followed a different interpretation of the transformative use test, which led to a settlement worth millions.

According to the settlement,

> EA's internal spreadsheets show that each avatar was matched to dozens of the real student-athlete's identifying characteristics . . . For example, for the NCAA football video game, EA matched: (1) the name of the real student-athlete; (2) his real-life jersey number; (3) his position played; (4) his hometown; (5) his year of eligibility; (6) his athletic abilities (on at least 22 dimensions, including speed, strength, agility, etc.); (7) his physical characteristics (on at least 26 dimensions, including, weight, height, skin color, face geometry, hair style, muscle shape, etc.); and (8) how he dressed for games in real life (on at least 28

dimensions, including shoes, how they taped, braces worn, undershirts, facemask and helmet styles, etc.).[106]

Though the courts were divided and prepared to deem Hart's case transformative in the Third Circuit based on user ability to further edit players, the settlement allowed EA Sports to escape further legal problems as they abandoned college sports video games altogether. The inconsistent line of decisions once again exposes the danger of protecting right of publicity through individual state laws that can vary.

Right of Publicity in Music, Celebrity, and Political Imitations

Sports video games are not the only arena where the industry runs into right-of-publicity issues. In fact, more frequently than with athletes, musicians and other celebrity likenesses are adapted into video game characters without permission.[107] The mutually beneficial licensing provisions of professional sports leagues limit right-of-publicity actions, but other industries do not typically collectively bargain away personal identity rights.

In one of the first right-of-publicity actions by a musician against a video game company, Keirin Kirby sued Sega in 2006 for a Japanese video game where a character looked and dressed like Kirby and used Kirby's catchphrase "ooh la la."[108] Sega prevailed in a California court because differences between the character and her real-life inspiration were deemed sufficiently "creative and transformative."[109]

More recently, however, Activision settled a case with No Doubt where the band posed for detailed avatars for the game *Band Hero*.[110] No Doubt's music was properly licensed to Activision and the company had permission to use No Doubt's likenesses in the game. The right-of-publicity issue arose when No Doubt accused Activision of going beyond the scope of their licensing agreement by allowing players to use No Doubt's likeness to perform songs that the band did not want to be associated with.[111] Ultimately, No Doubt avoided confronting First Amendment expression protections because the avatars used in the game were exact replicas of No Doubt.[112] As a result, there was no transformative use.[113] The case proved that even when proper licenses are obtained, right-of-publicity liability might still occur in interactive video game worlds depending on the scope of the licenses.

Celebrity and political images can be subject to right-of-publicity claims as well. In *The Last of Us*,[114] Naughty Dog released a main character named Ellie who looked and sounded like actress Ellen Page.[115] Recognizing legal trouble on the horizon, the company quickly revised the character so as to avoid an uncertain legal result under the transformative use test as established tentatively in *Hart* and other cases.[116]

Call of Duty is one of the most successful first-person shooting games of all time, with over 250 million sales as of January 2016.[117] The game features incredibly realistic gameplay that attempts to replicate the experience of war. In *Call of Duty: Advanced Warfare*,[118] Activision hired Kevin Spacey to voice a character named Jonathan Irons. Using performance capture technology, the game successfully copied Spacey's likeness to a highly recognizable degree.[119]

In 2014, however, the *Call of Duty* franchise almost took their realism too far. From a Panamanian prison, General Manuel Noriega sued Activision under right-of-publicity law for a character that was alleged to be a replica of the former dictator. Because video games are granted the same protections as books and movies, and because political speech is generally afforded greater First Amendment protections, the court concluded that the war criminal's publicity rights could not be more important under a balancing test than the protected, expressive content that gave rise to the action.[120]

Ultimately, right-of-publicity laws in video games offer a variety of case-by-case interpretations that fluctuate from district to district and state to state. Because it is difficult to guess how a court will interpret the multitude of tests, statutes, and common law precedence that governs this area of law, alleged violations could result in multimillion-dollar decisions or findings of no liability, depending on the courtroom and the state. Vagaries in right-of-publicity law and First Amendment rights of expression could produce a sobering effect that confounds the purposes of intellectual property law.

Moreover, the video game industry continues to evolve. In the last few decades, advancements in gaming system hardware capabilities and innovations in graphics have led to unprecedented levels of realism in video games. When applied to right-of-publicity actions, a radically evolving industry meets ambiguous laws with nearly unpredictable results. Until the courts balance First Amendment rights, fair use claims, and the rights of individuals, video game developers must continue to take calculated risks in the projects they choose to pursue.

Fortunately, the immense popularity and profitability of successful video games appears to justify the necessary risks in production, even without clear protection from the law. Although developers have been driven out of college sports and a handful of catastrophic lawsuits involving musicians and celebrities have resulted in large payouts, the video game industry continues to flourish. For now, the effect of inconsistent law has been minimal and isolated to a few instances where the risk was not worth the reward. Video game systems continue to become more realistic, however, and right-of-publicity issues will likely plague developers until more uniform policy emerges.

First Amendment and Censorship[121]

We also have seen video games giving rise to issues under the First Amendment. *Brown v. Entertainment Merchants Association*, 564 U.S. 08–1448 (2011) is considered a landmark case by the U.S. Supreme Court that reviewed a 2005 law from California that banned the sale of certain violent video games to children. Associations of companies that create, publish, and distribute video games sought a declaratory judgment to strike down the law. The district court found in favor of the associations and prevented the enforcement of the law. The U.S. Court of Appeals for the Ninth Circuit affirmed, holding that

> (1) violent video games did not constitute "obscenity" under the First Amendment, (2) the state did not have a compelling interest in preventing psychological or neurological harm to minors allegedly caused by video games, and (3) even if the state had a compelling interest, the law was not narrowly tailored enough to meet that objective.[122]

The U.S. Supreme Court subsequently struck down the law on the grounds that video games are considered protected speech under the First Amendment:

> Like the protected books, plays, and movies that preceded them, video games communicate ideas—and even social messages—through many familiar literary devices (such as characters, dialogue, plot, and music) and through features distinctive to the medium (such as the player's interaction with the virtual world). That suffices to confer First Amendment protection.

The First Amendment bars a state from restricting the sale of violent video games to minors.[123] Although obscene materials can be regulated from minors, violence is not considered obscene.

What is also interesting is the Court acknowledged that minors are entitled to First Amendment rights and that states can adopt laws to protect minors, "but that does not include a free-floating power to restrict ideas to which children may be exposed."[124] This is fairly important, and Justice Scalia included classics as an example of violence in reading:

> Certainly the *books* we give children to read—or read to them when they are younger—contain no shortage of gore. Grimm's Fairy Tales, for example, are grim indeed. As her just desserts for trying to poison Snow White, the wicked queen is made to dance in red hot slippers 'till

she fell dead on the floor, a sad example of envy and jealousy.' [. . .] Cinderella's evil stepsisters have their eyes pecked out by doves. And Hansel and Gretel (children!) kill their captor by baking her in an oven. High-school reading lists are full of similar fare. Homer's Odysseus blinds Polyphemus the Cyclops by grinding out his eye with a heated stake . . . In the *Inferno*, Dante and Virgil watch corrupt politicians struggle to stay submerged beneath a lake of boiling pitch, lest they be skewered by devils above the surface. And Golding's *Lord of the Flies* recounts how a schoolboy called Piggy is savagely murdered *by other children* while marooned on an island.[125]

The California law focused on the "interactive" nature as a distinguishing factor. But Justice Scalia again points to "choose-your-own-adventure" stories, starting in 1969. Justice Alito did a great deal of research to show that violence in video games is "astounding."[126] Justice Scalia took this one step further:

To what end does he relate this? Does it somehow increase the 'aggressiveness' that California wishes to suppress? Who knows? But it does arouse the reader's ire, and the reader's desire to put an end to this horrible message. Thus, ironically, Justice Alito's argument highlights the precise danger posed by the California Act: that the *ideas* expressed by speech—whether it be violence, or gore, or racism—and not its objective effects, may be the real reason for governmental proscription.[127]

Because video games are classified as protected speech, the law is reviewed under strict scrutiny, which is to say freedom-of-speech protections trump unless the law "is justified by a compelling government interest and is narrowly drawn to serve that interest."[128] Scalia found that under this demanding standard (which rarely allows for the regulation of speech), the California law did not satisfy the requirements. The state could not show a causal link between the violence in video games and harm to minors. Moreover, the voluntary rating system fills the needs of the concerned-parents control.

And finally, the Act's purported aid to parental authority is vastly over-inclusive. Not all of the children who are forbidden to purchase violent video games on their own have parents who *care* whether they purchase violent video games. While some of the legislation's effect may indeed be in support of what some parents of the restricted children actually want, its entire effect is only in support of what the State thinks parents *ought* to want. This is not the narrow tailoring to "assisting parents" that restriction of First Amendment rights requires.[129]

California was not the only state to have such laws, which had been overturned in Michigan and a bill defeated in Louisiana. The labeling system for games was put in place by the Entertainment Software Rating Board (ESRB) in 1994 as a self-regulating system that allowed parents and children to be able to evaluate the nature of the game and also prevent age-inappropriate materials being sold to minors without parental consent. The rating system remains voluntary, even though some in Congress in 2005 wanted to make it mandatory.[130] In 2011, the Federal Trade Commission conducted a study recruiting undercover 13- to 16-year-olds to try to buy R-rated materials (including movies, CDs, and video games) without a parent. Only 13 percent of the children were able to purchase electronic games (down from 20 percent in 2009 when the same study was conducted), compared to 38 percent for R-rated DVDs, 30 percent for R-rated movies, and 64 percent for R-rated music CDs.[131]

This case stands for a number of key elements: video games are protected First Amendment speech; violence is not defined as "obscene," unprotectable speech; and minors have a First Amendment right.

Notes

1. Mark Donatiello and John Billiris contributed to the writing of this chapter.
2. *Debbie Does Dallas*. Dir. David Buckley. School Day Films, 1978. Film.
3. Nintendo of Am., Inc. v. Dragon Pac. Int'l, 40 F.3d 1007. 9th Circuit 1994; Frosty Treats Inc. v. Sony Computer Entm't Am. Inc. 426 F.3d 1001. 8th Circuit 2005; Anti-Monopoly, Inc. v. Gen. Mills Fun Grp., Inc. 684 F.2d 1316. 9th Circuit 1982; Midway Mfg. Co. v. Bandai-Am., Inc., 546 F. Supp. 125. D.N.J. 1982; Morrison Entm't Grp. Inc. v. Nintendo of Am., Inc., 56 F. App'x 782. 9th Circuit 2003; Sega Enterprises Ltd. v. Sabella, No. C 93–04260 CW, 1996 WL 780560. Northern District of Cal. 1996; M. Kramer Mfg. Co. v. Andrews, 783 F.2d 421. 4th Circuit 1986; Incredible Techs., Inc. v. Virtual Techs., Inc., 400 F.3d 1007. 7th Circuit 2005; E.S.S. Entm't 2000, Inc. v. Rock Star Videos, Inc., 547 F.3d 1095. 9th Circuit 2008.
4. E.S.S. Entm't 2000, Inc. v. Rock Star Videos, Inc. 547 F.3d 1095, 1101. 9th Circuit 2008.
5. *Grand Theft Auto*. DMA Design. ASC Games, 1997. Multiple platforms.
6. Ibid.
7. Ibid. at 1097.
8. Ibid. at 1099.
9. Ibid. at 1100.
10. Ibid.
11. A reasonable consumer would not think a company that owns one strip club in East Los Angeles, which is not well known to the public at large, also produces a technologically sophisticated video game like San Andreas. E.S.S. Entm't 2000, Inc. v. Rock Star Videos, Inc., 547 F.3d 1095, 1100–01. 9th Circuit 2008.
12. Mil-Spec Monkey, Inc. v. Activision Blizzard, Inc., 74 F. Supp. 3d 1134, 1136. Northern District California 2014.

13. Ibid. at 1144.
14. *Call of Duty Ghosts*. Infinity Ward/Neversoft/Raven Software. Activision, 2013. Multiple platforms.
15. Mil-Spec Monkey, Inc. v. Activision Blizzard, Inc., 74 F. Supp. 3d 1134, 1143. Northern District California 2014.
16. Ibid. at 1144.
17. This section is written by Mark Donatiello.
18. Quinn, Gene. "What Is a Patent and Where Do Patent Rights Come From?— IPWatchdog.com|Patents & Patent Law." *IPWatchdogcom Patents Patent Law What Is a Patent and Where Do Patent Rights Come from Comments*. N.p., 20 February 2016. Web. 05 Mar. 2016, http://www.ipwatchdog.com/2016/02/20/what-is-a-patent-where-do-patent-rights-come-from/id=66345/.
19. Quinn, Gene. "What Is a Patent and Where Do Patent Rights Come From?— IPWatchdog.com|Patents & Patent Law." *IPWatchdogcom Patents Patent Law What Is a Patent and Where Do Patent Rights Come from Comments*. N.p., 20 February 2016. Web. 05 Mar. 2016, http://www.ipwatchdog.com/2016/02/20/what-is-a-patent-where-do-patent-rights-come-from/id=66345/.
20. "Using Patents to Generate Revenue in a Difficult Video Game Market." *Welts Journal Intellectual Property* 20.1 (2013): n. pag. *Westlaw*. Web., http://www.mwe.com/files/Publication/646cb2d3–4ddc-41ae-be84–82077a53db66/Presentation/PublicationAttachment/3f6da93a-8e1c-4660-bb42–84e02ad1a289/WLJ_INT2001_Commentary_Shaikh.pdf.
21. Bloomberg, Mark, and Steven Baughman. "Patents and the Video Game Industry: What You Don't Know Could Hurt You." *Patents and the Video Game Industry: What You Don't Know* (n.d.): n. pag. *Gamasutra*. Ropes and Gray's. Web, https://www.ropesgray.com/files/upload/02022011_Baughman_gamasutra.pdf.
22. Shaikh, Ahsan A. "Legal Games: Infringement Suits Hit the Social Gaming Sector." *Forbes*. Forbes Magazine, 30 July 2012. Web. 05 Mar. 2016, http://www.forbes.com/sites/ciocentral/2012/07/30/legal-games-infringement-suits-hit-the-social-gaming-sector/#171a8a9e6c39.
23. UltimatePointer, LLC v. Nintendo Co., Ltd. 2013 WL 6253767. Eastern District Texas. 2013.
24. Shaikh, Ashan A., Emery McDermott, and Will McDermott. "Using Patents to Generate Revenue in a Difficult Video Game Market." *Intellectual Property* (n.d.): n. pag. 01 May 2013. Web. 13. https://www.mwe.com/~/media/files/thought-leadership/publications/2013/05/using-patents-to-generate-revenue-in-a-difficult__/files/wlj_int2001_commentary_shaikh/fileattachment/wlj_int2001_commentary_shaikh.pdf
25. "Nintendo." |. N.p., n.d. Web. 03 Mar. 2016, https://www.nintendo.com/corp/legal.jsp.
26. "Copyright Law of the United States of America." *U.S. Copyright Office*. United States Copyright Office, n.d. Web. 03 Mar. 2016. www.copyright.gov
27. Chang, Steve, and Ross Danenberg. "Introduction." (n.d.): n. pag. *Banner & Witcoff, Ltd*. Banner & Witcoff. Web.
28. Atari Games Corp. v. Nintendo of Am. Inc. 975 F.2d 832. Federal Circuit 1992.
29. "Doctrine of Equivalents." *Legal Information Institute*. Cornell University Law School, n.d. Web. https://www.law.cornell.edu/wex/doctrine_of_equivalents
30. Ibid.
31. Garcia, Louis. "12 Unbelievable Video Game Patents You Didn't Know Existed." *GamesRadar+*. N.p., 20 May 2014. Web. 03 Mar. 2016. http://www.gamesradar.com/12-unbelievable-video-game-patents/

32. "Patent US4587200 — Photopolymerizable Composition Comprising an Acridine and a Heterocyclic Thiol Compound as a Photopolymerization Initiator and a Photographic Process Using Said Photopolymerizable Composition." *Google Books*. Google, n.d. Web. 03 Mar. 2016, http://google.com/patents/US4587200.
33. Garcia, Louis. "12 Unbelievable Video Game Patents You Didn't Know Existed." *GamesRadar+*. N.p., 20 May 2014. Web. 03 Mar. 2016. http://www.gamesradar.com/12-unbelievable-video-game-patents/
34. Ibid.
35. Ibid.
36. Narcisse, Evan. "Patents Show that the Next Xbox Might Be a DVR, Too." *Kotaku*. N.p., 03 Jan. 2012. Web. 03 Mar. 2016. http://kotaku.com/5872787/patents-show-that-the-next-xbox-might-be-a-dvr-too?comment=45669511
37. Shalkh, Ahsam A., Esq. "Using Patents to Generate Revenue in Difficult Video Game Market." *Intellectual Property* 20.1 (2013): n. pag. Westlaw Journal Intetllectual Property. McDermott Will and Emery, May 2013. Web. 03 Mar. 2016. https://www.mwe.com/~/media/files/thought-leadership/publications/2013/05/using-patents-to-generate-revenue-in-a-difficult__/files/wlj_int2001_commentary_shaikh/fileattachment/wlj_int2001_commentary_shaikh.pdf
38. Garcia, Louis. "12 Unbelievable Video Game Patents You Didn't Know Existed." GamesRadar+. N.p., 20 May 2014. Web. 03 Mar. 2016. http://www.gamesradar.com/12-unbelievable-video-game-patents/
39. Superannuation, "These Patents Video Game Publishers Own May Surprise You. Plus More..." Kotaku, September 6, 2013. Web 03 Mar. 2016. http://kotaku.com/these-patents-video-game-publishers-own-may-surprise-yo-511731513.
40. Ibid.
41. Ibid.
42. Ibid.
43. Ibid.
44. *Pong*. Atari. Atari, 1972. Coin operated.
45. Obias, Rudie. "11 Times Video Games Led to Lawsuits." *Mental Floss*. N.p., 2014. Web. 03 Mar. 2016. http://mentalfloss.com/article/55078/11-times-video-games-led-lawsuits
46. Ibid.
47. Obias, Rudie. "11 Times Video Games Led to Lawsuits." *Mental Floss*. N.p., 2014. Web. 03 Mar. 2016. http://mentalfloss.com/article/55078/11-times-video-games-led-lawsuits
48. Alpex Computer Corp. v. Nintendo Co., 102 F.3d 1214. Fed. Cir. 1996.
49. UltimatePointer, LLC v. Nintendo Co., Ltd. 2013 WL 6253767. Eastern District Texas 2013.
50. Frank, Allegra. "Activision Sued for Patent Infringement over Fantasy Sports Software (Update)." *Polygon*. N.p., 15 December 2015. Web. 05 Mar. 2016, http://www.polygon.com/2015/12/15/10222090/activision-blizzard-fantasy-sports-lawsuit-patent-infringement.
51. Ibid.
52. ProCD, Inc. v. Zeidenberg. 86 F.3d 1447. 7th Circuit 1996; Hill v. Gateway 2000, Inc. 105 F.3d 1147. 7th Circuit 1997; Davidson & Associates, Inc. v. Internet Gateway, Inc., 334 F. Supp. 2d 1164. Eastern District Montana 2004. aff'd sub nom; Davidson & Associates v. Jung, 422 F.3d 630. 8th Circuit 2005; Klocek v. Gateway, Inc., 104 F. Supp. 2d 1332. District Court Kansas 2000.

53. Allen v. Acad. Games League of Am., Inc., 89 F.3d 614. 9th Circuit 1996; Red Baron-Franklin Park, Inc. v. Taito Corp., 883 F.2d 275. 4th Circuit 1989.
54. *See In Re* Grand Theft Auto Video Game Consumer Litigation 416 F. Supp. 2d 1350 (2006)
55. MDY Industries, LLC. v. Blizzard Entertainment and Vivendi Games, Inc.
56. *Glider.* MDY Industries, 2005. Multiple platforms.
57. MDY Industries, LLC. v. Blizzard Entertainment and Vivendi Games, Inc.
58. This section is written by Mark Donatiello.
59. "Publicity." LII/Legal Information Institute, https://www.law.cornell.edu/wex/publicity.
60. Ibid.
61. *Restatement (Second) of Torts* §652 (1977).
62. "Publicity." *LII/Legal Information Institute*, https://www.law.cornell.edu/wex/publicity.
63. "Right of Publicity." *Right of Publicity RSS*, http://rightofpublicity.com/statutes/restatement-third-of-unfair-competition-s46–49#sthash.JO4lQh1q.aTCmAPkD.dpuf—See more at: http://rightofpublicity.com/statutes/restatement-third-of-unfair-competition-s46–49#sthash.JO4lQh1q.aTCmAPkD.dpuf.
64. "Right of Publicity." *Right of Publicity RSS*, http://rightofpublicity.com/brief-history-of-rop.
65. Coo, Andrew J.D. "Right of Publicity: The Right of Publicity Fair Use Doctrine—Adopting a Better Standard." *Buffalo Intellectual Property Law Journal* 4.1 (2006): 1–24. Web., http://buffaloipjournal.org/volumepdfs/biplj4121.pdf at 11.
66. Kwall, Roberta Rosenthal. "The Right of Publicity vs. the First Amendment: A Property and Liability Rule Analysist." *The Right of Publicity vs. the First Amendment: A Property and Liability Rule Analysist* (1994): n. pag. Web., http://ilj.law.indiana.edu/articles/70/70_1_Kwall.pdf at 47.
67. Coo, Andrew J.D. "Right of Publicity: The Right of Publicity Fair Use Doctrine—Adopting a Better Standard." *Buffalo Intellectual Property Law Journal* 4.1 (2006): 1–24. Web, http://buffaloipjournal.org/volumepdfs/biplj4121.pdf at 11.
68. The "actual malice" test suggests that when protected right-of-publicity elements are "inextricably entwined" with expressive content, the plaintiff must prove the use "intended to create the false impression in the minds of its readers" that the work viewed was the original image and not a manipulated, expressive one. The "actual malice" test has been criticized as being too narrow. Ibid. at 16.
69. The "transformative" test instead focuses on a fair use analysis, encouraging expression by determining whether the work in question "adds significant creative elements so as to be transformed into something more than a mere . . . likeness or imitation." The "transformative" test is widely criticized for being too narrow, failing to provide a clear standard, and problems in application when determining whether a work is sufficiently transformative.
70. Conversely, the "artistic relevance" test says that right-of-publicity laws are trumped by First Amendment expression in art "unless the [use of a celebrity name] has no artistic relevance to the underlying work whatsoever, or, if it has some artistic relevance, unless the [use] explicitly misleads as to the source of the content of the work." It is important to note that courts using the "artistic relevance" test use the same analysis in Lanham Act claims as in right-of-publicity claims. The "artistic relevance" test is criticized for providing too

much protection to artists and not considering any of the impacts on the individual suffering from the appropriation of his or her likeness. Ibid. at 17.
71. In addition to right-of-publicity analysis tests, the fair use doctrine may justify the appropriation of an individual's likeness. Many scholars call for a modified fair use defense that is particularly tailored to right-of-publicity issues to address First Amendment protection. As with copyright before it, the fair use doctrine might be able to strike a balance between First Amendment rights and individual rights of publicity in a way that inconsistent court tests have failed to do.
72. Kwall, Roberta Rosenthal. "The Right of Publicity vs. the First Amendment: A Property and Liability Rule Analysist." *The Right of Publicity vs. the First Amendment: A Property and Liability Rule Analysist* (1994): n. pag. Web., http://ilj.law.indiana.edu/articles/70/70_1_Kwall.pdf at 52.
73. Ibid.
74. *Death Race*. Exidy, Exidy, 1976. Coin operated.
75. *Tron*. Bally Midway. Bally Midway/ENCOM International, 1982. Coin Operated.
76. *Raiders of the Lost Ark*. Atari. Atari, 1982. Atari 2600.
77. Corriea, Alexa Rae. "E.T. Wasn't the Worst, or the First Video Game Based on a Movie." *Polygon*. N.p., 02 June 2014. Web. 04 Mar. 2016, http://www.polygon.com/2014/6/2/5762218/movie-based-games-e-t-atari.
78. Ibid.
79. *Star Wars: The Empire Strikes Back*. Atari. Atari, 1982. Atari 2600.
80. Corriea, Alexa Rae. "E.T. Wasn't the Worst, or the First Video Game Based on a Movie." *Polygon*. N.p., 02 June 2014. Web. 04 Mar. 2016, http://www.polygon.com/2014/6/2/5762218/movie-based-games-e-t-atari.
81. "The Design Evolution of Your Favorite Game Characters—Master Chief." *Complex*. N.p., n.d. Web, http://www.complex.com/pop-culture/2014/02/the-design-evolution-of-your-favorite-game-characters/master-chief.
82. MacArthur, Steven. "Gamasutra: Stephen McArthur's Blog—Right of Publicity in Video Games—How You Can Legally Include a Celebrity in Your Game." *Gamasutra Article*. N.p., 17 November 2014. Web. 04 Mar. 2016, http://gamasutra.com/blogs/StephenMcArthur/20141117/230361/Right_of_Publicity_in_Video_Games__How_You_Can_Legally_Include_a_Celebrity_in_Your_Game.php.
83. MacArthur, Steven. "Gamasutra: Stephen McArthur's Blog—Right of Publicity in Video Games—How You Can Legally Include a Celebrity in Your Game." *Gamasutra Article*. N.p., 17 November 2014. Web. 04 Mar. 2016, http://gamasutra.com/blogs/StephenMcArthur/20141117/230361/Right_of_Publicity_in_Video_Games__How_You_Can_Legally_Include_a_Celebrity_in_Your_Game.php.
84. Ibid.
85. Makuch, Eddie. "EA Hoping Its Add-On Content Sales Will Reach $1 Billion this Year." *GameSpot*. N.p., 26 August 2014. Web. 04 Mar. 2016, http://www.gamespot.com/articles/ea-hoping-its-add-on-content-sales-will-reach-1-bi/1100-6421932/.
86. MacArthur, Steven. "Gamasutra: Stephen McArthur's Blog—Right of Publicity in Video Games—How You Can Legally Include a Celebrity in Your Game." *Gamasutra Article*. N.p., 17 November 2014. Web. 04 Mar. 2016, http://gamasutra.com/blogs/StephenMcArthur/20141117/230361/Right_of_Publicity_in_Video_Games__How_You_Can_Legally_Include_a_Celebrity_in_Your_Game.php.

87. "Licensing." *Major League Baseball*. N.p., n.d. Web. 04 Mar. 2016, http://mlb. mlb.com/pa/info/licensing.jsp.
88. Ibid.
89. Ibid.
90. Lindbergh, Ben. "'MVP Baseball... 2015'? How the Best Baseball Video Game Ever Has Refused to Retire for 10 Years." *Grantland*. N.p., 14 April 2015. Web. 04 Mar. 2016, http://grantland.com/the-triangle/mvp-baseball-2005-mod-community-mlb-video-games/.
91. *MLB: The Show*. SCE San Diego Studio. Sony Computer Entertainment, 2006–2016. Playstation 2, Playstation 3, Playstation Portable, Playstation 4, Playstation Vita.
92. Lindbergh, Ben. "'MVP Baseball . . . 2015'? How the Best Baseball Video Game Ever Has Refused to Retire for 10 Years." *Grantland*. N.p., 14 April 2015. Web. 04 Mar. 2016, http://grantland.com/the-triangle/ mvp-baseball-2005-mod-community-mlb-video-games/.
93. *MVP Baseball*. EA Canada. Electronic Arts, 2005. Multiple platforms.
94. Lindbergh, Ben. "'MVP Baseball . . . 2015'? How the Best Baseball Video Game Ever Has Refused to Retire for 10 Years." *Grantland*. N.p., 14 April 2015. Web. 04 Mar. 2016, http://grantland.com/the-triangle/ mvp-baseball-2005-mod-community-mlb-video-games/.
95. *Madden*. EA Tiburon. EA Tiburon, 1988–2015. Multiple platforms.
96. Lindbergh, Ben. "'MVP Baseball . . . 2015'? How the Best Baseball Video Game Ever Has Refused to Retire for 10 Years." *Grantland*. N.p., 14 April 2015. Web. 04 Mar. 2016, http://grantland.com/the-triangle/ mvp-baseball-2005-mod-community-mlb-video-games/.
97. MacArthur, Steven. "Gamasutra: Stephen McArthur's Blog—Right of Publicity in Video Games—How You Can Legally Include a Celebrity in Your Game." *Gamasutra Article*. N.p., 17 November 2014. Web. 04 Mar. 2016, http://gamasutra.com/blogs/StephenMcArthur/20141117/230361/Right_of_ Publicity_in_Video_Games__How_You_Can_Legally_Include_a_Celebrity_ in_Your_Game.php.
98. Ibid.
99. Doe v. McFarlane. 208 S.W.3d 52. Montana Court of Appeals for the Western District 2006.
100. Ibid.
101. "NCAA, EA Sports to Pay $60mn to College Athletes for Using Likenesses in Video Games." *RT International*. N.p., 17 July 2015. Web. 04 Mar. 2016, https://www.rt.com/usa/310142-ncaa-video-game-settlement/.
102. Farrey, Tom. "Players, Game Makers Settle for $40M." *ESPN*. ESPN Internet Ventures, 31 May 2015. Web. 04 Mar. 2016, http://espn. go.com/espn/otl/story/_/id/11010455/college-athletes-reach-40-million-settlement-ea-sports-ncaa-licensing-arm.
103. "Keller v. Electronic Arts Inc. (In Re NCAA Student-Athlete Name & Likeness Licensing Litig.)." Web blog post. *Publication and News*. Loeb & Loeb LLP, n.d. Web. 2016.
104. Ibid.
105. Gutmann, Joseph. "It's in the Game: Redefining the Transformative Use Test for the Video Game Arena." *Cardozo Arts & Entertainment* 31 (2012): 215–48. Cardozo AELJ. Web. http://www.cardozoaelj.com/wp-content/uploads/2013/ 01/Gutmann-Its-In-the-Game.pdf

106. Farrey, Tom. "Players, Game Makers Settle for $40M." *ESPN*. ESPN Internet Ventures, 31 May 2014. Web. 2016. http://www.espn.com/espn/otl/story/_/id/11010455/college-athletes-reach-40-million-settlement-ea-sports-ncaa-licensing-arm
107. MacArthur, Steven. "Gamasutra: Stephen McArthur's Blog—Right of Publicity in Video Games—How You Can Legally Include a Celebrity in Your Game." *Gamasutra Article*. N.p., 17 November 2014. Web. 04 Mar. 2016, http://gamasutra.com/blogs/StephenMcArthur/20141117/230361/Right_of_Publicity_in_Video_Games__How_You_Can_Legally_Include_a_Celebrity_in_Your_Game.php.
108. Ibid.
109. Ibid.
110. *Band Hero*. Neversoft/Budcraft Creations/Vicarious Visions. Activision, 2009. Multiple platforms.
111. MacArthur, Steven. "Gamasutra: Stephen McArthur's Blog—Right of Publicity in Video Games—How You Can Legally Include a Celebrity in Your Game." *Gamasutra Article*. N.p., 17 November 2014. Web. 04 Mar. 2016, http://gamasutra.com/blogs/StephenMcArthur/20141117/230361/Right_of_Publicity_in_Video_Games__How_You_Can_Legally_Include_a_Celebrity_in_Your_Game.php.
112. Gutmann, Joseph. "It's in the Game: Redefining the Transformative Use Test for the Video Game Arena." *Cardozo Arts & Entertainment* 31 (2012): 215–48. Cardozo AELJ. Web. http://www.cardozoaelj.com/wp-content/uploads/2013/01/Gutmann-Its-In-the-Game.pdf
113. No Doubt v. Activision Publishing, Inc. Court of Appeals of California. 15 February 2011, WestLaw. Web.
114. *The Last of Us*. Naughty Dog. Sony Computer Entertainment, 2013. Playstation 3.
115. Chin, Kevin. "The Transformative Use Test Fails to Protect Actor—Celebrities' Rights of Publicity." *Northwestern Journal of Technology and Intellectual Property* 13.2 (2015): n. pag., September 2015. Web. http://scholarlycommons.law.northwestern.edu/cgi/viewcontent.cgi?article=1237&context=njtip
116. Ibid.
117. Skipper, Ben. "Call of Duty Franchise Tops 250 Million Sales Worldwide following Black Ops 3 Success." *International Business Times RSS. IBTimes Co., Ltd*, 15 January 2016. Web. 2016. http://www.ibtimes.co.uk/call-duty-franchise-tops-250-million-sales-worldwide-following-black-ops-3-success-1538166
118. *Call of Duty: Advanced Warfare*. Sledgehammer Games. Activision, 2014. Multiple platforms.
119. Suellentrop, Chris. "Casting the Single-Player Movie Star." *The New York Times*, 01 November 2014. Web. 2016. http://mobile.nytimes.com/images/100000003194156/2014/11/02/arts/video-games/kevin-spacey-stars-in-call-of-duty-advanced-warfare.html
120. McArthur, Stephen. "Right of Publicity in Video Games—How You Can Legally Include a Celebrity in Your Game." *Gamasutra: The Art & Business of Making Games*. N.p., 17 November 2014. Web. 2016. http://www.gamasutra.com/blogs/StephenMcArthur/20141117/230361/Right_of_Publicity_in_Video_Games__How_You_Can_Legally_Include_a_Celebrity_in_Your_Game.php
121. This section is written by Ron Gard and Elizabeth Townsend Gard.

122. Brown v. Entertainment Merchants Association. U.S. Supreme Court 27 June 2011. Oyez: Chicago-Kent College of Law at Illinois Tech. Web.
123. Ibid.
124. Ibid.
125. Ibid.
126. Ibid.
127. Ibid.
128. Ibid.
129. Ibid.
130. Another bill was introduced in 2012, HR 4204, to require warning labels, but it did not pass. See Higgins, Parker. "Warning: Exposure to Video Game Labeling May be Hazardous to Freedom of Speech." *EFF*, 22 March 2012, https://www.eff.org/deeplinks/video-games?page=0%2C3.
131. "FTC Undercover Shopper Survey on Enforcement of Entertainment Ratings Finds Compliance Worst for Retailers of Music CDs and the Highest among Video Game Sellers." *FTC Undercover Shopper Survey on Enforcement of Entertainment Ratings Finds Compliance Worst for Retailers of Music CDs and the Highest among Video Game Sellers*. N.p., 20 April 2011. Web. 05 Mar. 2016, https://www.ftc.gov/news-events/press-releases/2011/04/ftc-undercover-shopper-survey-enforcement-entertainment-ratings (last visited January 2016).

4   The Gaming Community and Fans[1]

Fans and the Law

Fans do many things that the law has not yet addressed. For example, they make copies; they make their own versions of games; they record themselves playing the games; they sell elements of the game in knitted versions on Etsy. In dedication to their games, fans regularly violate the letter of the law. Video game companies have approached these infringements in many different ways.

Early on, the video game industry had to think through the relationship they would have with their fans. Microsoft was one of the first to give their fans permissible uses for creating their own works, through their terms of use. It subsequently has become a model for others. They realized that fans were not the enemy, even if what they were doing violated traditional notions of copyright, trademark, and patent law. So began a concept of permissible uses—fan uses allowed by the content holders. Others, such as the MPAA (Motion Picture Association of America), would call them "tolerable" uses.

Among the most favorable legal tools for the fan is fair use. This is a concept appearing in the 1976 Copyright Act that allows certain uses to be deemed "not infringement." The question arises, however, as to which uses qualify. In this section, we look first at two fan creations—fan fiction and "let's play" videos—that particularly implicate questions of permissible and fair uses. Fans also love games long after they have commercial value and the companies that made them are marketing them. We therefore next examine the legal questions that arise when fans want to play these old games on new platforms not authorized by the copyright holder. We then turn to the latest issues of doxing and swatting, wherein fans get carried away and their real-world actions bring criminal laws to bear. Finally, we look at questions that have been raised regarding the use of fan labor.

Fan Fiction and Derivative Works

Since the invention of the Atari gaming console in the early 1970s, video games have become an integral part of our society's creative expression and enjoyment. Video games, although they differ from traditional creative media, represent immensely creative expressions of ideas on behalf of their creators. They are a conglomeration of animation, cinema, music, and storytelling. Like films, paintings, and literature, video games are likewise vulnerable to copying. Video games, therefore, are subject to the protections conferred by copyright law. Because of unique technological roadblocks, unauthorized reproductions are rare, though they still occur. These reproductions are most often seen in the form of emulators—software designed to re-create console games that may be downloaded illicitly from the Internet and played on one's computer. With the threat of actual reproduction being limited for authors of video games, the most important right conferred on those authors by copyright law is the derivative right.

Among the bundle of rights granted by U.S. copyright law is the right "to prepare derivative works based upon the copyrighted work."[2] The Copyright Act provides that a copyright proprietor holds the exclusive right to prepare derivative works based on a copyrighted work.[3] A derivative work is a work based on a preexisting work, for example, a video game based on a short story or a short story based on a video game.[4] Therefore, a derivative work is any work that relies substantially on the protected expressions of ideas in a preexisting work. The classic example of this would be a sequel. In a film or a novel, wherein protection extends not only to the story but also to the unique characters, the taking of those familiar characters and placing them in another story would constitute a derivative work. In the context of video games, sequels are commonplace. The wildly popular video game series *Final Fantasy*[5] has been replicated and adapted over sixty times to extend the concept's profitability. Although the characters and stories change from game to game, the essence of each game falls within the *Final Fantasy* brand, and each game may have relied on other protected elements outside of characters, such as the worlds where the story takes place. Because copyright law was intended to promote the creation of new works by protecting the pecuniary interests of those who create them,[6] the derivative right is in place to ensure the ensuing profitability of a successfully expressed concept is retained or controlled by the original author.

These rights belong to the copyright holder. Fans violate these rights by creating their own versions of the characters or game-related art. The right to make derivative works was originally limited, in practice, to ensuring creators of successful games the ability to exclusively create sequels and to control how and where the characters of those games were used. The derivative right arguably kept the Sega company in business well into the 1990s because of the company's exclusive control over the wildly popular game *Sonic the Hedgehog*.[7] Today, with the exponential growth in technological capabilities, the derivative right has become much more complicated. This new realm of user-generated content raises boundless copyright questions from "When is it acceptable to alter the content of a game you have purchased?" to "Who then owns the copyright to that altered content?"

User-generated content is nothing new to the gaming world. *Madden NFL '96*[8] offered gamers the ability to create their own player.[9] In 2000, Tony Hawk's *Pro Skater 2*[10] offered gamers the ability to design their own custom skate park and then use their character to skateboard in it.[11] These games represent the beginning of user-generated content. They mark the first instances of gaming companies acknowledging their customers' desire to interact on an even deeper level with the games they play. Today, that need has grown exponentially, and we have entire games premised around the concept of user-generated content.

Minecraft is a "virtual sandbox" game where there is essentially no mission, story, or objective outside of using the resources offered in the game to create things. This concept of a "sandbox" game where the underlying premise is to offer gamers the ability to unleash their imaginations by providing them with a digital toolkit has exploded.[12] Therefore, from the games where users were given the option to create their own content within specific parameters in a specific section of the game, we now have entire games that rely completely on user-generated content. From building a custom skatepark in which a custom skateboarder can ride, we now are able to build custom buildings, cities, and even worlds. Hello Games' *No Man's Sky*[13] is offering players the ability to edit entire planets.[14]

Players, however, are not simply making things within the games they play. Some are creating mods—modified versions of the game—that contain entire levels or change the gameplay completely. The concept of modding is similar to, yet different from, the user-generated content we've discussed thus far. Up to this point, we have only mentioned user-generated content that was intended by the game developers. However, mods represent user-made changes to an entire game. Perhaps the most popular example of this is the *Counter-Strike*[15] mod of the *Half-Life*[16] video game. *Half-Life* is a first-person shooter game, and the *Counter Strike* mod changed the way its multiplayer function works, creating a more team-oriented experience where one team plays the role of terrorists and battles another team playing the counterterrorists.[17] The mod drastically altered the original gameplay, but it became such a huge hit that millions of players preferred to play the mod over the original game.[18] From this, Valve Software, the developer for *Half-Life*, modified its distribution model to accommodate and embrace modding as part of the gameplay experience players are looking for.[19] Valve later released various *Counter Strike* variants that sold over 10 million copies, demonstrating just how lucrative modding can be.[20]

Two primary legal questions arise: Is user-generated content illegal, and does it infringe on copyright law? From a strict copyright law perspective, it does. Fans are making copies or derivative works from copyrighted works. But legal doctrine does not necessarily rule the day. Many companies have put in place terms of use that allow for user-generated content—nonexclusive licenses to make copies and create derivative works. From early on, Microsoft has been the leader in this area. As Don McGowan explained, the issue is one of interplay between promotion and protection. Companies are willing to allow fans to do lots of things with the brand, and as he put it, you have to be famous to get ripped off. Fans of video games feel a part of the experience, identifying with the characters they play. He predicts that courts may eventually acknowledge the participatory element of the creative process of fans.

Whereas some forms of user-generated content can be considered original expressions, a great deal more of the category likely falls under the realm of derivative works that are not copyrightable without the owner's permission.[21] Such derivative works could maintain protection as fair use. However, fair use is a defense that is convoluted at best and requires a heavy fact-based interrogation and is applied on a case-by-case basis. Furthermore, some games, including *World of Warcraft*, come with shrink-wrapped contracts listing the games as "walled gardens" immune to fair use.[22] The end user license agreement for *World of Warcraft* states that users "may not, in whole or in part, copy, photocopy, reproduce [. . .] or create derivative works based on the Game."[23] Moreover, in the context of mods, courts have interpreted them narrowly and categorized them as noncopyrightable derivative works.[24] For example, in *Micro Star v. Formgen Inc.* the court held that a series of maps created by a user was a derivative work not qualifying for fair use even though the code used to program the maps did not include any of the original game's code.[25]

Not all companies have been so strict regarding the policy for IP rights in user-generated content. The widely popular online game *Second Life*,[26] which allows users to interact in an immensely detailed digital world, grants its "residents" IP rights over their creations both in the virtual world and real life.[27] Because of the widespread use of user-generated content and the desire to avoid litigation, game companies have begun to address it in their terms of use. Activision addresses user-generated content in article 6 of its terms of use. It states that users creating their own content from its games grant Activision a perpetual, worldwide, royalty-free, nonexclusive license to use, reproduce, or create derivative works from the user-generated content.[28] Activision takes the license a step further and grants a similar license to all other users of the game once a player publicly posts his or her user-generated content.[29] Activision finishes by outlining types of user-generated content, which it retains the right to terminate, including harassing, abusive, sexually explicit, or generally vulgar material.[30] Insomniac Games has similar provisions in its terms of service, but provides a clause that explicitly deems that the copyright in the user-generated content is owned by its creator.[31]

Furthermore, companies have recently begun monetizing user-generated content for their players. Daybreak Games, the developer for the wildly popular massive multiplayer online role-playing game *Everquest*,[32] has recently launched its Player Studio.[33] The Player Studio is essentially a marketplace for gamers to create and sell items to be used in the game.[34] Players are able to create their own items, upload them to the marketplace (after Daybreak approves them), and sell them. Daybreak then pays the players 40 percent of the sale price.[35]

Valve Games also owns Steam, an online distribution platform that represents how the majority of computer gamers purchase their games.[36] After embracing modding as a policy, the company has recently turned Steam into a way for fans to monetize their creations. Valve announced in 2015 that it was releasing a platform for modders to sell their mods on Steam.[37] Valve had experimented with a program similar to Daybreak's Player Studio that allowed users to sell their cosmetic items in the games *Team Fortress 2*[38] and *Dota 2*[39] in 2011.[40] The program was considered a huge success, as it paid out $57 million to content creators in the community over the four years from 2011 to 2015.[41]

By creating distribution and monetization methods for mods and other forms of user-generated content, gaming companies have conceded that content editors and creators within the games own at least a share of the rights to their creations. However, when looking to find the industry's true stance on who owns the copyright to user-generated content, the best place to look is in a development company's terms of use.

In a world where games are easily modified by enthusiastic players from their own computers and then quickly disseminated across the globe, gaming companies have had to adapt their strategies. There is an across-the-board acknowledgement that user-generated content represents (typically) an original creation that merits individual copyright protection vesting in its author. However, development companies have protected themselves by granting themselves nonexclusive rights to the content. Furthermore, many companies are finding ways to monetize these consumer-created contributions, both for themselves and the consumers. This process represents a compromise that pleases both sides, as the users are free to continue creating their mods and profit from them, but the development companies retain their pecuniary rights in the games that inspire these mods.

Further legal issues arise with 'machinima.' Machinima is a word that has been coined to describe the newly popular method of creating films through the use of video games. Machinima filmmakers use a video game's engine as the setting and characters for their films. They play the video game in a way that brings life to their characters, while capturing the gameplay in a digital recording. They then edit that recording like film, dubbing in dialogue and music. The final result is an animation-esque film made almost entirely from content within the video game.

The most popular piece of machinima is the Internet television series *Red vs. Blue*,[42] made by machinima company Rooster Teeth. *Red vs. Blue* is a series made from the game *Halo*, an outer space first-person shooter game, which comedically mocks the nature of first-person shooter games. *Red vs. Blue* has seen tremendous success and is considered the pioneer in the field as it is now available on Netflix.

The laws governing machinima are closely tied to the laws concerning user-generated content, as previously discussed. After all, machinima can be thought of as the stepchild of user-generated content. It represents game users taking the games they play and adapting them for a more interactive experience. As previously stated, the goal of copyright law is to benefit society by encouraging the creation of new works of literature and art.[43] Using video game engines to produce films is precisely the sort of innovation one would expect the copyright laws to protect.[44]

Although there is yet to be a lawsuit filed by a game developer against a machinima filmmaker, machinima films will almost always constitute derivative works. First, a machinima film is based upon the game it uses as its animation and could not exist without that game.[45] Second, machinima movies may be considered "abridgments" of the games they use, and "abridgments" are expressly listed as derivative works in the 1976 Copyright Act.[46] Machinima films also could be considered "elaborations" and classified as derivative works by the same act.[47] Finally, courts have held that editing clips of a film to make a preview for that film constitutes a derivative work.[48] This is the most closely analogous process to machinima that has received treatment by the courts to date.

The only saving grace machinima filmmakers may find is the fair use defense. *Red vs. Blue* likely would be considered a parody because it used a first-person shooter game to comment on the nature of first-person shooter games. However, not all machinima films will have such a clear-cut defense. The other films likely would need to rely on "transformation" as its primary reason for fair use. An infringing use of copyrighted material may be considered transformative if "it adds new material to the original work and gives it a further purpose or different character, altering the [original] with new expression, meaning, or message."[49] This factor likely would play in favor of machinima because it takes an existing work, a video game, and adds dialogue, story, and character beyond what is originally presented. Furthermore, it presents the work in an entirely new form: a film. However, some commentators have suggested that a transformative work is still derivative if it creates a new work for a different market.[50] There is no conclusive stance among experts as to whether machinima is appealing to a new market.[51]

Fair use also considers four distinct factors. The first is whether the work in question is commercial, as commercialized works will be less likely to avail themselves of a fair use defense.[52] The second factor is the "nature of the copyrighted work."[53] Whether this factor plays in favor of the machinima filmmaker will depend on whether the portion of the copyright owner's work that was used by the filmmaker is more factual or more fictional.[54] Because a machinima filmmaker is using expressive and protected assets of the video game, this factor likely would cut against a notion of fair use. The third factor is "the amount and substantiality of the portion used in relation to the copyrighted work as a whole."[55] If the machinima film consists mostly of the game developer's protected material without much addition of new material, this factor will weigh against fair use.[56] Machinima filmmakers would argue that they have added dialogue, a storyline, and a new essence to the existing characters that may be entirely different from the way they were originally presented. This factor could be interpreted either in favor of or against fair use. The fourth factor is "the effect of the use upon the potential market for or value of the copyrighted work."[57] This factor could be interpreted to favor either side. Development companies would argue that machinima is free-riding on the existing popularity of the games they use to appeal to the same market, which could be seen as a potential market development companies would like to explore. Machinima filmmakers could claim that video game development companies have existed for forty years without seeking to explore this market, which is evidence that the markets are separate and unaffected by each other. It is difficult to predict how a court would weigh this factor.

The fair use defense for machinima filmmakers therefore is murky at best. For precisely this reason, an attorney for *World of Warcraft* developer Blizzard Games advised machinima creators not to rely on the fair use defense when planning their films.[58]

However, many game developers see machinima in a positive light. Even Blizzard, which is known for imposing tight restrictions on its players' rights to use and adapt its games and for attempting to contract players out of a fair use defense with its end user agreements, has opened its doors to machinima.[59] Many game developers see machinima as an art form that is harmless, at worst, and, at best, constitutes great publicity for their brand. Microsoft addresses machinima in its game content usage rules. In these rules, Microsoft states that it supports use of machinima for noncommercial purposes only.[60] It does, however, have an explicit exception for ad-driven revenue from sites like YouTube.[61] Blizzard, on the other hand, omits this exclusion for ad-driven revenue from the videos it allows.[62] However, Blizzard states that "as long as the website that hosts your Production provides a free method to allow viewers to see the Production, Blizzard Entertainment will not object to your Production being hosted on that site."[63] Blizzard seems to be prohibiting machinima videos made from its games to be shown on subscription-based or pay-to-view based websites or channels. It is possible, then, that machinima filmmakers would be within their rights to post their videos to YouTube and receive ad revenue from it.

Ultimately, machinima marks uncharted territory in the legal realm. As game developers realize that those who make these films and the audiences they are reaching are most often their greatest fans, litigation has been avoided. Thus we have seen the promotion of such creations in user agreements. Furthermore, many companies are welcoming licensing arrangements for machinima filmmakers who seek to commercialize their films. Rooster Teeth, the production company responsible for *Red vs. Blue*, has a licensing deal with Microsoft, which has provided an email address for any filmmakers to contact the corporation about licensing opportunities.[64] Therefore, the solutions seem to be found before litigation is necessary.

'Let's Play.' Video Games and Copyright[65]

The world of gaming is dynamic. Not only are people recording themselves playing games ('"Let's Play' videos), but the trend is now to livestream, watching others playing video games. Chat windows allow players and their audience to interact. One can give shout-outs in real time. The gaming industry is encouraging all of this. What would have been strict infringement has become condoned and encouraged as part of the game. But the video game industry very early on recognized the value of their fans interacting and creating derivative works. Today, gaming companies partner with YouTube and Twitch to more seamlessly allow use of their materials by fans.

The legal definition of a 'Let's Play' is not something easily explained; rather, the term itself has grown and transformed from what it was originally intended to be. The first 'Let's Play' was more akin to a "let us play"[66] and involved a community member of the 'Something Awful Forum' asking other members to play with them. At its inception, it was about the content creator playing with the audience,[67] although this has changed a lot over the past nine years. The supposed first video 'Let's Play,'[68] also originating on the 'Something Awful Forum,' was of a game called *The Immortal*[69] by a user known as 'Slowbeef.' It was initially a screenshot 'Let's Play', but the user decided to add video supplements as he completed the game, and thus began what has now became an online phenomenon.

On January 4, 2007, the first 'Let's Play' was created. However, as has been previously mentioned, this concept has become altered throughout the past number of years; it is no longer only a complete play-through of a game with commentary. The YouTube channel known as 'Let's Play,' which was created by the production company Rooster Teeth,[70] is evidence of this. This is not to say that a 'Let's Play' cannot be a full play-through of a game, but instead shows that the term has become broader, allowing for a greater range of content to be included within this category. It now can be used to refer to longer-form gameplay videos that include live audio recorded along with the gameplay. In today's form of 'Let's Play,' it is this live commentary aspect that is seen as granting the video the title.

The original 'Let's Plays' were essentially a single person completing an entire game in stages, with some measure of commentary. These types of video subsequently have become known as 'walkthroughs.' However, there also are shorter-form videos, showing specific strategies, known as 'guides.'[71] Additionally, there are other styles of gameplay videos that fall into neither the category of a 'Let's Play' nor a 'guide.' An example of these comes from the YouTube channel 'Funhaus.'[72] The creators of this channel do not have a short-form title for the style of their videos, but they liken their style of gameplay videos to that of the television series *Mystery Science Theater 3000*.[73] It is clear that the term 'Let's Play' encompasses a number of different definitions, as there are many different opinions of what constitutes a 'Let's Play.'[74] However, no matter the definition, the legal issues that pertain to them are the same.

Copying the game is traditionally seen as a violation of copyright. The question is whether the content owner—the holder of the copyright—has given permission in their terms of use to violate copyright and, if they have not, whether fair use from the 1976 Copyright Act covers the uses of "Let's Play" videos. In other words, the main question to be answered with regard to 'Let's Plays' and other gameplay videos is whether the content creators have the right to use the video games in the course of their 'Let's Plays.' Some companies explicitly state that their games can be used in this way. Some content owners allow derivative uses, including 'Let's Play' videos. The main stipulation included by these developers is that the content cannot be locked behind a 'paywall.'[75] This does not mean that the creator cannot profit from these videos; rather, it provides that the creator cannot charge viewers to watch the content. What is permitted is participation in the 'Partnership Program' on YouTube[76] or the equivalent on Twitch.tv. This regulation is echoed by other companies, such as Ubisoft.[77]

Nevertheless, there are still those companies that do not believe that 'Let's Plays' and other gameplay videos are covered by fair use and that they are not transformative. These companies possess the view that they are derivative works, and thus they should be compensated for them. The largest proponent of this view is the company Nintendo. This company is exceptionally protective of its properties and views any 'Let's Plays' containing their content as derivative works. As such, they enforce a strict policy when it comes to 'Let's Plays.' Until January 2016, their policy required creators to register their channel with Nintendo, who would then take a portion of all of the ad revenue generated from all of the videos on the channel, whether they contained Nintendo works or not.[78] However, this has now changed, as it became clear to Nintendo that they retained no rights over videos that did not contain content from their games. Nintendo's updated policy requires content creators to remove videos from the registered channel if the game titles in the video are outside of their list of supported games.[79] Although some argue that Nintendo fails to understand YouTube[80] and its users, this action is still within their rights, as they own the properties. Yet policies such as these do nothing but stifle innovation in an emerging field.

Old Games, Copyright, and the DMCA Section 1201 Exemptions[81]

Some video game fans argue that old video games should go into the public domain faster. One project, called "Full Screen Mario," re-created all of *Super Mario Bros.*[82] and allowed users to create their own levels in the game. However, in November 2013, Nintendo took it down, citing copyright infringement. The original game, created in the 1980s, is not nearly old enough to go into the public domain.[83] Outdated technology alone is not enough to force a game into the public domain by current U.S. copyright laws. In fact, for most of those games, the copyright will last ninety-five years from publication. So what does one do when they want to play a game that has become obsolete? What if it was on a platform that no longer is provided by the game maker? For this, one must turn to part of the Copyright Act, Section 1201, which seems to be one way to allow the playing of games long after the company who made the game stops supporting its still-under-copyright work.

Every three years, the Copyright Office takes requests on what exemptions to allow regarding circumventing technology. The first example was film professors being allowed to take snippets of films to create compilations for their classes and needing to be able to circumvent technology on

DVDs in order to do that. Fans of older games wanted to be able to continue to play online multiplayer games after they no longer were supported by the video game company. The game company previously had set up a network to allow players to communicate with each other. When the company stopped supporting the game, the players wanted to keep playing. The game companies did not want the players to reverse engineer or crack encryption. They argued that they should continue to have control over who gets access to their multiplayer games, and therefore they should be able to enforce authentication control over the players. The game companies suggested that libraries or archives could preserve copies. But the players wanted to *play* the games, not preserve them. The game companies fought very hard to keep the exception from being adopted by the Copyright Office. Betsy Rosenblatt, a law professor specializing in video games and user-generated content, believes this may be an issue we see develop more significantly over time.

Rosenblatt explained,

> We see that [companies] get very upset with competing fan games or content that is inconsistent with the vision of the games' brand. So, while most of the time the game companies and fan communities are on the same side, they diverge sharply when someone wants to make sexually explicit machinima, or that sort of thing. Because that is not what the game companies want to be associated with.

Game players won a small victory in 2015 when the Copyright Office allowed an exemption for video game archiving. Kendra Albert from EFF described this allowance as

> an exemption for the circumvention of authentication servers in order to render games playable, so long as the game content is stored on the player's computer or console. There's now more legal protection for modifying a single player game where the authentication server has been deactivated for continued play or for preservation. So if and when Blizzard deactivates those *Diablo III* servers, players can modify their own games to continue playing.[84]

The exemption covers "local gameplay," requiring the gameplay to be on a personal computer or video game console and not through an online service. That allows for local multiplayers but not online multiplayers. Libraries, museums, and archives can "eliminate access controls on video game consoles (often called 'jailbreaking') in order to copy or modify games to get them running again after a server shutdown."[85]

The Dark Side of Fans: Doxing and Swatting

The experiences of women and sexual minorities in gaming comprise another issue raised by Rosenblatt. As she notes, "A huge percentage of avid gamers are women, gay, trans, and yet, there is a culture of exclusion that has really targeted those people." She feels that gaming culture needs to change to be more inclusive, but that these matters have been met with fear and resistance by the dominant male segment of the culture. She sees exclusion on many levels, from gaming experiences to game creation. She particularly is concerned with the phenomenon of 'doxing' (the releasing of someone's personal documents and outing someone's real-life name in order for others to persecute them) and 'swatting' (Internet pranking of emergency services). Rosenblatt notes that doxing cases haven't yet gone to court, but she asks the troubling question: "Who do you get a restraining order against? The world?"

Both doxing and swatting are real crimes. Swatting consists of someone calling 911 or filing a false police report that a crime has been committed—a murder or bomb threat, for example—in order to provoke the police to investigate and raid an individual's house or business. Swatting targets those who are livestreaming their game playing sessions in order to allow the audience watching to see the SWAT team arrive. Criminal penalties have been imposed for swatting. In 2014, a fifteen-year-old gamer, Paul Homer, swatted and was convicted of domestic terrorism, with a sentence of twenty-five years to life in federal prison. He was the first person to be charged and convicted of swatting. Swatting is a fad among gamers, as they seek to find out personal information about other gamers: "they will call in a dangerous threat to law enforcement and watch as the 'livestreamer's house is forcibly entered by the police."[86] In the case of Homer, he made a call to 911, claiming, "I just shot and killed four people. If any police enter my home I will kill them too." The judge did not take the prank lightly: "Leave your petty pride in the realm of digital fantasy where it is still safe. [. . . A]ctions in the real world don't have a reset button. And every parent should make sure their children understand that."[87] Homer is not the only teen to be caught swatting. In May 2015, a seventeen-year-old hacker in British Columbia pleaded guilty to extortion, false police reports, and criminal harassment. In this case, the gamer had been targeting women when denied friend requests in *League of Legends*. In response, he shut down their Internet access, posted their personal information online, and called them repeatedly. He also told the police that he was holding a family hostage or that he had killed someone and to send SWAT teams to victims' homes. These two examples are illustrative, but others exist. A University of Arizona student, for example, withdrew from the university due to threats from a hacker who called the police, claiming he was holding the student's father and brother at gunpoint.[88]

Gamer/Fan Labor and Right of Publicity

One issue that is arising is the concept of fan labor and whether allowing fans to create new mods, 'Let's Play' videos that serve as advertising for the game, and other derivative works is, in fact, exploitative. Rosenblatt is also quick to point out that video game companies are very receptive to fan creations, but only to a point, especially when fans begin to crack copyright protection and encryption on their consoles. We have also seen great resistance to fans being allowed to break encryption to preserve games that are no longer formally supported.

Right-of-publicity issues are affecting fans. Mike Monohan, an attorney in Chicago, who also teaches video game law at the Illinois Institute of Technology's Chicago-Kent College of Law, had the experience of having his virtual identity and events from his gaming life re-created in a comic book without his permission.[89] Monohan, a highly active player in the game *Eve*, became the unwitting basis for a comic book story. Such curious remediations raise a number of interesting questions: What does it mean to be playing in a game? What kind of right of publicity do gamers have over the characters/avatars/roles they create? When a comic book company sets out to attribute dialogue, use your online character, and sell comics, what kind of intellectual property rights of the player are infringed upon? Do players have property rights in their gameplay and in their personalities? Who owns the story of the player in the game? Many terms-of-use agreements say that the game company owns all the game content, but do they own the player's actions within the game? In other words, where does game content end and personality/experience begin?[90]

Notes

1. Karl Craig and Mitch Longan contributed to the writing of this chapter.
2. A "derivative work" is a work based upon one or more preexisting works, such as a translation, musical arrangement, dramatization, fictionalization, motion picture version, sound recording, art reproduction, abridgment, condensation, or any other form in which a work may be recast, transformed, or adapted. A work consisting of editorial revisions, annotations, elaborations, or other modifications which, as a whole, represent an original work of authorship, is a "derivative work." 17 U.S.C.A. § 106.
3. Value Group, Inc. v. Mendham Lake Estates, L.P. 800 F.Supp. 1228, 24. District New Jersey 1992.

4. 17 U.S.C.A. § 101.
5. *Final Fantasy* (franchise). Square Enix (formerly SquareSoft). Square Enix (formerly SquareSoft), 1987–2015. Multiple platforms.
6. U.S. Const. art. I, § 8, cl. 8.
7. *Sonic the Hedgehog*. Yuji Naka, Naoto Ohshima, and Hirokazu Yasuhara. Sega, 1991. Sega Genesis.
8. *Madden NFL '96*. Tiburon Entertainment/High Score Productions. EA Sports, 1995. Multiple platforms.
9. "Top 25 Features in Madden NFL History." *Top 25 Features in Madden NFL History*. N.p., 02 August 2015. Web. 05 Mar. 2016, https://www.easports.com/madden-nfl/news/2013/madden-football-history.
10. *Pro Skater 2*. Neversoft. Activision, 2000. Multiple platforms.
11. "Create-A-Park." *Tony Hawk's Games Wiki*. N.p., n.d. Web. 05 March 2016, http://tonyhawkgames.wikia.com/wiki/Create-A-Park.
12. "How Will User-Generated Content Affect the Future of Video Games?—." N.p., n.d. Web. 03 Mar. 2016, http://modsquad.com/how-will-user-generated-content-affect-the-future-of-video-games/
13. *No Man's Sky*. Hello Games. Hello Games, 2016. Playstation 4, Microsoft Windows.
14. "How Will User-Generated Content Affect the Future of Video Games?—." N.p., n.d. Web. 03 Mar. 2016, http://modsquad.com/how-will-user-generated-content-affect-the-future-of-video-games/
15. *Counter-Strike* (franchise). Valve Corporation/Turtle Rock Studios/Hidden Path Entertainment/Gearbox Software/Ritual Entertainment/Nexon. Valve Corporation/Sierra Entertainment/Namco/Nexon, 1999–2012. Multiple platforms.
16. *Half-Life* (franchise). Valve Corporation/Gearbox Software. Sierra Entertainment/Valve Corporation, 1998–2007. Multiple Platforms.
17. "Counter-Strike Mod for Half-Life." *Mod DB*. N.p., n.d. Web. 03 Mar. 2016, http://www.moddb.com/mods/counter-strike.
18. "Computer Game Mods, Modders, Modding, and the Mod Scene | Scacchi | First Monday." *Computer Game Mods, Modders, Modding, and the Mod Scene | Scacchi | First Monday*. N.p., n.d. Web. 03 Mar. 2016, http://www.firstmonday.org/article/view/2965/2526.
19. Ibid.
20. Ibid.
21. 14 Int'l J. Comm. L. & Pol'y 1.
22. Ibid.
23. Ibid.
24. Micro Star v. Formgen Inc. 154 F.3d 1107. 9th Circuit 1998.
25. Ibid.
26. *Second Life*. Linden Labs, 2003–2015. Microsoft Windows, OS X, Linux.
27. 14 Int'l J. Comm. L. & Pol'y 1.
28. "Activision | Terms of Use." *Activision | Terms of Use*. N.p., n.d. Web. 03 Mar. 2016, http://www.activision.com/legal/terms-of-use.
29. Ibid.
30. Ibid.
31. "Terms of Service—Insomniac Games." *Insomniac Games*. N.p., n.d. Web. 03 Mar. 2016, http://www.insomniacgames/terms-of-service.

32. *Everquest.* Sony Online Entertainment. Sony Online Entertainment, 1999. Microsoft Windows, OS X.
33. "Player Studio—Daybreak Games." N.p., n.d. Web, https://player-studio.day breakgames.com.
34. Ibid.
35. Ibid.
36. "Whoa, Valve Just Monetized Mods." *Motherboard.* N.p., n.d. Web. 03 Mar. 2016, http://motherboard.vice.com/read/whoa-valve-just-monetized-mods.
37. Ibid.
38. *Team Fortress 2.* Valve Corporation. Valve Corporation, 2007–2013. Multiple Platforms.
39. *Dota 2.* Valve Corporation. Valve Corporation, 2013. Microsoft Windows, OS X, Linux.
40. "Whoa, Valve Just Monetized Mods." *Motherboard.* N.p., n.d. Web. 03 Mar. 2016, http://motherboard.vice.com/read/whoa-valve-just-monetized-mods.
41. Ibid.
42. *Red vs. Blue.* Dir. Burnie Burns. Rooster Teeth Productions, 2003–2016. Internet Series.
43. U.S. Const., art. I, § 8, cl. 8.
44. Matthew Freedman, Note: Machinima and Copyright Law, 13 J. Intell. Prop. L. 235, 238. http://digitalcommons.law.uga.edu/cgi/viewcontent.cgi?article=1319& context=jipl
45. Ibid. at 245.
46. 17 U.S.C.A. § 101.
47. Ibid.
48. Video Pipeline, Inc. v. Buena Vista Home Entm't, Inc., 192 F. Supp. 2d 321, 331, 62 U.S.P.Q.2d (BNA) 1464, 1468–69. District New Jersey 2002, dismissed by Video Pipeline, Inc. v. Buena Vista Home Entm't, Inc., 210 F. Supp. 2d 552. District New Jersey 2002. aff'd Video Pipeline v. Buena Vista Home Entm't, 2003 U.S. App. LEXIS 17757. 3rd Circuit N.J. 2003.
49. Campbell v. Acuff-Rose Music, Inc. 510 U.S. 569, 578. Supreme Court 1994.
50. Paul Goldstein, Copyright § 5.3.1 (2d ed. 1996).
51. Matthew Freedman, Note: Machinima and Copyright Law, 13 J. Intell. Prop. L. 235, 238.
52. Harper & Row, Publishers, Inc. v. Nat'l Enters., 471 U.S. 539, 562 (1985).
53. 17 U.S.C. § 107.
54. Matthew Freedman, Note: Machinima and Copyright Law, 13 J. Intell. Prop. L. 235, 238 citing Campbell at 586. http://digitalcommons.law.uga.edu/cgi/viewcontent.cgi?article=1319&context=jipl
55. 17 U.S.C. § 107.
56. Campbell at 588.
57. 17 USCS § 107.
58. "How to Make Machinima without Getting Sued Blind." *Gigaom.* N.p., n.d. Web. 03 Mar. 2016, https://gigaom.com/2009/04/28/how-to-make-machinima-without-getting-sued-blind/.
59. "Blizzard Video Policy." *Blizzard Entertainment.* N.p., n.d. Web. 03 Mar. 2016, http://eu.blizzard.com/en-gb/company/legal/videopolicy.html.
60. "Game Content Usage Rules." *Game Content Usage Rules.* N.p., n.d. Web. 03 Mar. 2016, http://www.xbox.com/en-us/developers/rules.
61. Ibid.

62. "Blizzard Video Policy." *Blizzard Entertainment.* N.p., n.d. Web. 03 Mar. 2016, http://eu.blizzard.com/en-gb/company/legal/videopolicy.html.
63. Ibid.
64. "How to Make Machinima without Getting Sued Blind." *Gigaom.* N.p., n.d. Web. 03 Mar. 2016, https://gigaom.com/2009/04/28/how-to-make-machinima-without-getting-sued-blind/.
65. This section is written by Karl Craig.
66. "Did I Start Let's Play?" *Slowblr—.* N.p., n.d. Web. 03 Mar. 2016, http://slow beef.tumblr.com/post/41879526522/did-i-start-lets-play.
67. Ibid.
68. This is not stated as fact, as there is no real way to prove this. Other content creators claim to have come up with the term; however, this is the theory with the most support due to the timestamps on the forum post.
69. *The Immortal.* Sandcastle. Electronic Arts, 1990. Multiple Platforms.
70. Rooster Teeth, N.p., n.d. Web., https://roosterteeth.com/.
71. These can range from how to complete a specific task or mission to how to obtain an item in the game.
72. Funhaus. "Funhaus." *YouTube.* YouTube, n.d. Web. 05 Mar. 2016, https://www.youtube.com/channel/UCboMX_UNgaPBsUOIgasn3-Q.
73. Funhaus, "Fine Bros STOP REACTING?—Dude Soup Podcast #55." *YouTube.* YouTube, n.d. Web. 05 Mar. 2016, https://www.youtube.com/watch?v=8EPN4 4aAchs&list=PLbIc1971kgPDJjVdQcLZZz4Exygpo2cuB&index=4.
74. McConnell, Fred. "Let's Play—the YouTube Phenomenon That's Bigger than One Direction." *The Guardian.* Guardian News and Media, 02 January 2014. Web. 05 Mar. 2016, http://www.theguardian.com/technology/2014/jan/02/lets-play-youtube-pewdiepie-one-direction.
75. *Supra* notes 39 and 40.
76. *YouTube.* YouTube, n.d. Web. 05 Mar. 2016, https://www.youtube.com/yt/creators/get-started.html?noapp=1 (last visited February 29, 2016, 04:21 pm).
77. http://forums.ubi.com/showthread.php/773563-Ubisoft-policy-on-YouTube-videos-Forums (last visited February 29, 2016, 04:19 pm).
78. Tassi, Paul. "Nintendo Updates Their Bad YouTube Policies By Making Them Worse." *Forbes.* Forbes Magazine, n.d. Web. 05 Mar. 2016, http://www.forbes.com/sites/insertcoin/2015/02/06/nintendo-updates.
79. Ibid.
80. Ibid.
81. This section is written by Alexandra Stork and Ron Gard. Interview conducted by Elizabeth Townsend Gard with Betsy Rosenblatt.
82. *Super Mario Bros.* (franchise). Nintendo R&D4. Nintendo, 1985–2013. Multiple platforms.
83. Lee, Timothy B. "Nintendo Says this Amazing Super Mario Site Is Illegal. Here's Why It Shouldn't Be. (Updated)." *Washington Post.* The Washington Post, 17 October 2013. Web. 03 Mar. 2016. https://www.washingtonpost.com/news/the-switch/wp/2013/10/17/nintendo-says-this-amazing-super-mario-site-is-illegal-heres-why-it-shouldnt-be
84. Albert, Kendra. "The New DMCA §1201 Exemption for Video Games: A Closer Look." *Electronic Frontier Foundation.* EFF, 13 November 2015. Web. 03 Mar. 2016. https://www.eff.org/deeplinks/2015/11/new-dmca-ss1201-exemption-video-games-closer-look
85. Ibid.

86. Gogol, Bryan. "15 Year Old Who "SWATTED" Gamer Convicted of Domestic Terrorism; 25 Years to Life in Federal Prison." *National Report RSS*. National Report, 30 August 2014. Web. 03 Mar. 2016. http://nationalreport.net/15-year-old-swatted-domestic-terrorism/

87. Ibid.

88. Jacobs, Harrison. "Teenage Hacker Admits to Stalking and 'Swatting' Female Gamers Who Turned Him Down." *Business Insider*. Business Insider, Inc., 22 May 2015. Web. 03 Mar. 2016. http://www.businessinsider.com/lizard-squad-hacker-was-just-arrested-for-swatting-female-league-of-legends-gamers-2015-5

89. Mike's experience with the game *Eve* was re-created in Dark Horse comics. He only found out he was in a comic when it came out, and his character, Tayler Link, came to personify the Goonswarm side of a massive war. Mike made the whole experience into an exam question on how the right-of-publicity issues would play out had he objected.

90. Don McGowan first told us this story, and then we had the pleasure of interviewing Mike himself.

5 Employment[1]

According to many employees within the industry, the majority of new employees, especially those mid- and entry-level workers, find out quickly that the job is seemingly too good to be true.[2] Many video game employee practices are not up to par with other technological businesses and thus not upholding the standards as other technology companies have. Many lower- and mid-level employees are subjected to harsh work environments, which include long hours, very little pay, no job benefits, little to no job security, and slim chances for promotion in the future.[3] The video game sector has even harsher implications for minorities such as women and racial minorities, where they make up a small percentage of the overall field and are not as generally accepted. Consequently, they are not a unionized labor force, which makes them vulnerable to not only harsh industry standards, but also nonprofit groups such as the IGDA (International Game Developers Association), who are more interested in pushing their own agendas than providing a stable employment sector to their workers.[4]

The main problem within the video game employment sector is the exploitation of employees through the inhumane working conditions. Employees lack job security, especially those who are recent college graduates and who hold entry-level jobs. The now-defunct publication *Game Developer Magazine* in a survey found that 12 percent of the respondents have been laid off in 2012, which is twice as high as the national mass layoff rate that year.[5] In their study they uncovered that many companies have horrid policies, such as mass hiring in entry-level positions during big projects and then firing those entry-level positions during downtimes after those projects have been completed.[6] For example, the video game company Red Storm hired the majority of their entry-level employees as temporary workers. Most of them were young college graduates who were paid minimum wage. Because they were temps, they had no benefits and they were subjected to being fired at will without notice, even though many of them had been promised by higher management within the company that they could work toward permanent employment. Unfortunately, they were laid off en masse without warning after the project was completed.[7]

On the contrary, many smaller companies hire very few workers, and they exploit and overwork employees when projects arise instead of hiring extra help. This process is known in the gaming world as "crunch time," when employees are called to work more hours during a project to complete it on time. During this time, employees, on average, work six or seven days in a row and between sixty-nine and eighty hours a week. These entry- to mid-level workers, on average, are paid minimum wage or just above, and they oftentimes are not compensated for overtime.[8] This was brought to national attention in 2006, when the wife of one of the employees from the company Electronic Arts (EA) posted an anonymous blog entitled "EA: The Human Story" to shed light on these practices by describing the reality behind the video game façade that video game companies foster.[9] Her blog post detailed the long hours, poor compensation, and stressful work conditions that programmers across the industry experienced, underscoring that video game workers want and need a balance between professional and personal lives.[10]

These types of practices, once brought to the forefront of mainstream media, were socially condemned. Moreover, they became the subject of the two lawsuits brought against EA in 2006. Both class action lawsuits were settled outside of court for an estimated 30 million dollars.[11] In the first suit, the plaintiffs (who remained anonymous to protect their job security in the industry) brought action, saying that EA violated California's overtime law.[12] Although EA claimed that all the workers who worked overtime were exempt from overtime pay because they were quid pro quo employees and they would need to be reclassified in order to get overtime unless they gave up their stock options, they still settled outside of court, giving rise to advocates of video game employees, who believe that these draconian practices violate employment law.[13] To try to curtail the use of these sorts of work conditions after settling, EA and other big video game companies began exploring strategies such as a taskforce of video game spouses who became watchdogs to ensure that video game employees weren't overworked and severely underpaid. However, once the media attention faded, many companies reverted to poor working conditions, and these conditions continue to exist today. For example, in a survey conducted in 2015, crunch time dropped from 2.2 percent of video game workers not having crunch time in 2004 to 19 percent not having crunch time within a two-year period. Crunch time periods at work also dropped from 35 percent working sixty-five to eighty hours to 38 percent in 2004 to 38 percent working fifty to sixty-nine hours in 2015.[14] Companies are starting to acknowledge that although crunch time is the cheapest way to meet a deadline, it is a practice that generates bad press. Unfortunately, there is still a long road ahead, as two-fifths of video game employees are still working in a toxic crunch-time work environment, and in 2010 video game company Rockstar faced similar claims of exploitation of employees only four years after EA settled out of court.[15]

One aspect that may be changing is unionization. As video games cross over into entertainment, the unions (e.g. the Actors' Guild, the Writers Guild) see as problematic the lack of unionization within the video game industry. The current lack of artist unionization causes labor practices to be uncertain. Unionization would bring stability—health care, for example—and potentially move the video game industry toward traditional, linear media business practices.

Discrimination against minorities and especially against women represents another prevalent problem within the video game employment sector. According to the IGDA, women make up only about 11.5 percent of the video game employment sector, which means that this sector is vastly gender imbalanced.[16] Additionally, within this 11.5 percent of women in the industry, very few hold senior positions with these companies. Many explain this by way of the stereotype of gamers not including females. The 1990s saw a big push to bring women in to work on game development staffs for major companies.[17] This movement largely failed, however, because women breaking into the field didn't receive adequate support. Yet, some headway was made by women finding employment within gender-neutral games such as the *Sims*, with this being seen as a "compromise" regarding gender equality.[18] Many developers also discriminate against women who have comparable employment experience as well as education to their male counterparts under the ruse that they want a candidate who will either have a passion for play or previous experience in the industry, which is hard for females breaking into this field to obtain. Some females face sexism as they try to advance in the field. Because the video game industry dominantly markets to men, managers oftentimes operate with a perception that women won't be able to make sound judgments when it comes to building video games for men.[19] Females also have a harder time getting promoted in this field. According to *Forbes*, a $9,000 annual pay gap exists between men and women who work comparable positions within the field.[20]

Although women in the video game industry very seldom have been able to bring a claim of gender discrimination under the U.S. legal system, former Microsoft security program manager Katherine Moussouris alleged in a 2015 lawsuit that the company's employee review system discriminates against women in performance evaluations, compensation, and promotions. "Microsoft's company-wide policies and practices systematically violate female technical employees' rights and result in the unchecked gender bias that pervades its corporate culture," the complaint reads. "The disadvantage to female technical employees in pay and promotion is not isolated or exceptional, but rather the regular and predictable result of Microsoft's policies and practices and lack of proper accountability measures to ensure fairness."[21] Microsoft CEO Satya Nadella became a lightning rod for this issue when he said last year that women should not explicitly ask for a raise, but rather rely on "good karma."[22] He later apologized and said he misspoke.[23] Moussouris was paid less than her male counterparts throughout her tenure at the company, the suit contends. The suit cites multiple instances in which she received lower ratings than her manager said she deserved and was passed over for deserved promotions, including once when she was on maternity leave.

Finally, the video game sector's failure to unionize has become a prevalent problem because it is a factor in the continuation of exploitation of video game company employees. The closest entity to a union that exists for employees is the nonprofit organization IGDA. This organization doesn't include middle or lower management or entry-level employees. It continuously "self-promotes" its organization as an educational tool to be utilized by employees to ensure that the work environment is pleasant.[24] However, many laborers and institutions disclosed in a survey that the organization is highly insufficient and doesn't tend to the needs of the workers, but instead pushes the agendas of upper management. In this survey, 50 percent of workers don't want anything to do with the IGDA,[25] whereas the other 50 percent want more enforcement of fair and humane policies and, without that enforcement, views the organization as feeble.[26] A former president of the IGDA exclaimed in a board meeting that he agreed with the draconian practice of making workers work over sixty hours and sometimes more than eighty during crunch time.[27] He also agreed with mass hiring and firing, as well as temporary vast relocations of employees and their families.[28]

Although the world of video games and employers has been substantially progressing since 2004, there is still a long way to go before their customs and standards are anywhere near on par with employment practices elsewhere in the technology field.

Notes

1. Markeecha Forcell contributed to the writing of this chapter.
2. Statistics come from *Game Developer Magazine* that folded under Gamasutra; these statistics were gathered in 2012. Williams, Ian. "You Can Sleep Here All Night: Video Games and Labor." 13 September 2013, https://www.jacobinmag.com/2013/11/video-game-industry/
3. Statistics from 2013 from IGDA annual report; Williams, Ian G. "Crunched: Has the Games Industry Really Stopped Exploiting Its Workforce?" 18 February 2015,

http://www.theguardian.com/technology/2015/feb/18/crunched-games-industry-exploiting-workforce-ea-spouse-softwarey.

4. Statistics come from *Game Developer Magazine* that folded under Gamasutra, these statistics were gathered in 2012. Williams, Ian. "You Can Sleep Here All Night: Video Games and Labor." 13 September 2013, https://www.jacobinmag.com/2013/11/video-game-industry/

5. Ibid.

6. Ibid.

7. Statistics come from *Game Developer Magazine* that folded under Gamasutra, these statistics were gathered in 2012. Williams, Ian. "You Can Sleep Here All Night: Video Games and Labor." 13 September 2013, https://www.jacobinmag.com/2013/11/video-game-industry.

8. Ibid.

9. Williams, Ian G. "Crunched: Has the Games Industry Really Stopped Exploiting Its Workforce?" 18 February 2015, http://www.theguardian.com/technology/2015/feb/18/crunched-games-industry-exploiting-workforce-ea-spouse-softwarey.

10. Chmielewski, Dawn C. "EA Agrees to Settle Overtime Lawsuit." *LA Times*, 26 April 2006, http://articles.latimes.com/2006/apr/26/business/fi-ea26.

11. Ibid.

12. Wingfield, Nick. "Electronic Arts Settles Lawsuit, Will Pay Overtime for Some Jobs." *Wall Street Journal*, 06 October 2005, http://www.wsj.com/articles/SB112854591447960878.

13. Williams, Ian. "You Can Sleep Here All Night: Video Games and Labor." 13 September 2013, https://www.jacobinmag.com/2013/11/video-game-industry/

14. Ibid.

15. "Rockstar Spouses Allege 'Degrading' Work Conditions at San Diego Kris." *Pigna Studio*, 09 January 2010, http://www.1up.com/news/rockstar-spouses-allege-degrading-work.

16. Dyer-Withelford, Nick, and Greig De Peuter. "EA Spouse & Crisis of Video Game Labour: Enjoyment, Exclusion, Explanation, and Exodus." *CTC Canadian Journal of Communication* 31.2 (2006), http://cjc-online.ca/index.php/journal

17. Ibid.

18. The complaint is embedded into the article. Rao, Leena. "Microsoft Hit with Gender Discrimination Lawsuit." 16 September 2015, http://fortune.com/2015/09/16/microsoft-gender-discrimination-suit/

19. dyer withelford, Nick, and Greig De Peuter. "EA Spouse & Crisis of Video Game Labour: Enjoyment, Exclusion, Explanation, and Exodus." *CTC Canadian Journal of Communication* 31.2 (2006), www.ctc.com.

20. Ibid.

21. Rao, Leena. "Microsoft Hit with Gender Discrimination Lawsuit." 16 September 2015, http://fortune.com/2015/09/16/microsoft-gender-discrimination-suit/

22. Ibid.

23. Ibid.

24. Williams, Ian. "You Can Sleep Here All Night: Video Games and Labor." 13 September 2013, https://www.jacobinmag.com/2013/11/video-game-industry.

25. Ibid.

26. Ibid.

27. Ibid.

28. Ibid.

6   Legal Issues With eSports[1]

Legal issues are arising related to eSports a term that is short for electronic sports and has come to be associated with describing video game competitions. Much like traditional sports, both amateur and professional scenes exist for the sports in question here. Likewise, eSports has teams, contracts, leagues, and sponsorships. Esports are very early in their lifespan, however, and thus the legal infrastructure is not yet as well developed in many ways as traditional sports. Visas, for example, are routinely denied to competitors to go to events because they do not fit the traditional definition of an athlete or businessman[2]; specific contracts between players and teams are kept secret with unethical strategies being used[3]; and the basic terms of these contracts also are slanted heavily in favor of the organization, with players unable to argue for better conditions.[4]

This lack of infrastructure, direct precedent, and general lack of legal knowledge on the parts of players, organizations, and, to an extent, the companies is likely the cause behind all of the issues that exist in the eSports scene. It must be stressed that there is very little scholarly research done about eSports even less so in legal scholarship.

Esports has been growing in size year after year. In terms of viewership, for instance, the largest eSports event of 2015 was the *League of Legends* LCS 2015 with over 36 million unique viewers and a peak of 14 million concurrent viewers worldwide.[5] The prize pool for the event was $US2.13 million. The second largest event, called the International 2015, an eSports event featuring the game *Dota 2*, had a peak of 4.6 million viewers and an $US18 million prize pool.[6] Championship matches for LCS and the International have filled up entire sports stadiums, and smaller events still are able to fill large convention spaces. These statistics are not very surprising in light of the fact that over 150 million Americans play video games, with more than half of all households owning some sort of dedicated games console and 40 percent of Americans indicating that they play three hours or more of video games each week.[7] Of course, these statistics are not directly translatable to eSports because the study did not specify between eSports titles and non-eSports titles. The study, for instance, did not differentiate between individuals who played video games on mobile devices (phones, tablets) as opposed to traditional gaming devices (portable, home, personal computer). Of the largest eSports titles in terms of revenue, sponsorship, and prize money, the vast majority of them are only available on personal computers[8] (*League of Legends, Dota 2*, and *Starcraft II*[9] are all personal computer–exclusive games), so it stands to reason that there may not be a direct correlation between the figures.

Nevertheless, the size of the eSports industry is hard to deny, even when it is evaluated separately from the gaming industry as a whole. According to SuperData research, the eSports industry generates around $US748 million in sponsorships, pro-players, ticket sales, gambling, merchandising, ticket sales, and other direct revenue.[10] This figure does not include game sales, sales of downloadable content, or microtransactions (i.e., in-game payments, which can offer direct benefits in the game, most often in mobile games, such as the ability to purchase extra plays in *Candy Crush*[11]); it looks only at the revenue that eSports directly generate through competitions.

Esports unquestionably are a large industry in their own right, as shown by the $US748 million figure, but that large figure does not include the amount of money that the companies themselves are making from the heavy promotion of the game itself. According to SuperData Research, for instance, Riot Games generated $1.3 billion in revenue from microtransactions alone in 2014 from *League of Legends*.[12] *Dota 2* sold a digital item referred to as the Compendium, a promotional item for the International tournament. In addition to in-game benefits, 25 percent of the revenue generated from sales of the Compendium went toward increasing the prize pool of the International tournament, with a base starting amount of $US1.6 million.[13] By the time the Compendium sales were completed, the tournament prize pool was in excess of $US18 million,[14] and this is not including the amount of money *Dota 2* generated from its in-game microtransactions, which is its primary method of generating revenue. (These numbers are not released because Valve is a private company.)

Esports are usually looked at as a whole when comparing them with other industries.[15] However, eSports consist of many different individual games, with each game being its own esport. When a sequel of the game comes out, typically the eSports scene (i.e., tournaments, players, sponsorships) moves to the new game. One example of this is *Street Fighter V*.[16] After being released in February 2016, it has replaced *Street Fighter IV*[17] on the lineup of games to be played at this year's EVO. (EVO is the largest fighting game tournament, with nine games being played in a three-day event in Las Vegas, with a variable prize pool that last year was in excess of $300,000.)[18] However, the esport itself is referred to as *Street Fighter*. A helpful analogy would be the fact that the NFL changes its rules every so often, thus creating a "new" version of football each time it is done. Some exceptions to sequels replacing the old games exist; for instance, *Super Smash Brothers Melee*[19] has a higher viewership, sponsorship level, and prize money than its successor, *Super Smash Brothers for Wii U*.[20] (Colloquially referred to as *Smash 4*.)

Unlike traditional sports, eSports themselves are software that some entity has copyright control over. No individual or entity owns football, for instance, so theoretically one could organize a football tournament and no one could stop the tournament on the basis of the organizers not having the rights to the game. Originally, Blizzard Entertainment (the creators of *Starcraft*[21]) found it more difficult to restrict Korean broadcasting of games and tournaments.[22] When the successor to *Starcraft*, *Starcraft II*, was released, the game could not be played without a direct connection to Blizzard, thus allowing Blizzard to control licensing more directly.[23] This mistake has not been repeated by *League of Legends*, in which the game cannot be played offline, thus allowing Riot to have complete control over the game. Interestingly enough, both *Counter-Strike Global Offensive* and *Dota 2* can be played on local area networks (allowing for non-Internet multiplayer gameplay on multiple computers) and are owned by Valve Entertainment. However, this likely ties into Valve's business strategy with these two games, which relies heavily on community-generated content.

Proprietary control is very important when it comes to eSports. Many gaming companies have learned from the mistakes of Blizzard Entertainment, who was unable to control KESPA (Korean Esports Association, which was responsible for organizing pro players, granting licenses, scheduling showtimes on Korean television, etc.[24]) for many years and as a result did not receive a portion of the direct revenue generated from the *Starcraft Brood War*[25] eSports scene.[26] For the most part, all of the largest tournaments are now sponsored and funded by the companies themselves. The International is funded by Valve, LCS is funded by Riot, and the *Starcraft II* World Championship is funded by Blizzard with broadcasting rights being leased to several different Korean companies.[27] Nearly all of these games have their largest tournaments broadcast on Twitch.tv, an online streaming website that allows people to watch gameplay footage in real time. Because of the primarily online distribution of eSports content (with the exception of South Korea), this furthermore allows the companies not to have to rely on other broadcasting companies to show their tournaments. (Indeed, streaming has become so lucrative that YouTube is beginning to expand their streaming capabilities for games.[28])

Third-party eSports leagues are being brought into line, but instead of shutting them down, they allow them to continue with a license. A great example of this occurred with the Super Smash Brothers community. In 2013, EVO was sent a cease-and-desist letter by a lawyer at Nintendo, stating that they were not allowed to broadcast *Super Smash Brother Melee*.[29] However, after online backlash, especially considering that *Melee* had been a staple at EVO for years, Nintendo reversed its decision.[30] To this day there are those who believe that this decision was actually made in error, given that the decision was immediately reversed and no such decision was made before; there is a suspicion that the lawyer may simply have been new and didn't know what he was doing. Regardless, after the EVO 2013 incident, Nintendo started to reach out to tournament organizers and sponsored them. In 2014 and 2015, Nintendo not only licensed broadcasting rights to MLG (Major League Gaming), EVO, APEX 2015 (the premier Smash tournament where all versions of the game are played), and many other leagues, but also sponsored the events, providing money, equipment, and promotion on their Twitter and Facebook pages.

Leasing and sponsoring the tournament also had other benefits for Nintendo. A fan-made modification to *Super Smash Brothers Brawl*,[31] referred to as *Project M*,[32] was very popular and featured in many tournaments.[33] However, because *Project M* was not a Nintendo product, not only did they not receive money from it (it was a free download, but the makers received donations), but it also created a product that could potentially compete with their products. When Nintendo began to sponsor these tournaments, *Project M* disappeared from the event listings in its entirety. Although this cannot definitely be linked to Nintendo, it is very likely that *Project M*'s omission was a stipulation by Nintendo for sponsorship. In 2015, the makers of *Project M* ceased their development of the mod in its entirety. The reason, they claim, was not because they were targeted by any legal action by Nintendo, but rather because they saw it as a potential hurdle in the future.[34]

Third-party leagues are becoming more valuable as well, as their production companies, industry knowledge, and connections make them very valuable to both investors and gaming companies. It also allows for the company to have more control over their eSports presence. In 2015, ESL (Electronics Sports League) was acquired by a Swedish media company for $US87 million because the company saw the worth in the future.[35] In 2016, MLG was purchased by Activision-Blizzard for a rumored $US46 million in order to better promote their eSports titles. (These include, among others, *Starcraft*, *World of Warcraft*, *Call of Duty*, *Heroes of the Storm*,[36] and *Hearthstone: Heroes of Warcraft*.[37]) By absorbing the league, it is able to better control the tournament. Another example can be seen in how Nintendo sponsors tournaments. At these tournaments, the traditional commercial break, where an ad would be run on the streaming website (usually Twitch.tv) instead was replaced with Nintendo commercials and promotions. (Nintendo brought a setup of a demo version of the then-unreleased game *Splatoon*[38] for attendees to play at Apex 2015.[39]) Greater company involvement and control allow for greater control of the message.

A potentially interesting issue that could have a large impact on the eSports scene is the idea of copyrighting concepts and game mechanics. It is well established in copyright law that you cannot copyright archetypes and settings.[40] For example, although you can copyright Spider-Man, you cannot copyright the idea of a superhero who has spider-based powers in New York City. It appears that this principle also applies to game mechanics, although it is untested in the realm of video games.

The Copyright Office statement on this matter seems pretty succinct.[41] The "methods of playing a game" are unprotected according to the statement and "similar methods" may be used. This is consistent with the history of several eSports titles. An example that highlights this is the history of *DotA*, *League of Legends*, *Heroes of Newerth*,[42] *Heroes of the Storm*, and *Smite*.[43] The original *DotA* was a fan modification developed by several enthusiasts for *Warcraft III: Reign of Chaos*.[44] Over time, the developers split up to pursue their own projects. Guinsoo would end up creating *League of Legends*, and Icefrog was hired by Valve to create *Dota 2*. *Heroes of Newerth* was a game that had similar game mechanics as the other two and also was derived from the original *DotA*.[45] With the popularity of what was then called *DotA*-style games arising, other companies jumped into the mix. Blizzard created a game known as *Blizzard DotA*, and Hi-Rez studios created *Smite*. All of these games retained elements from *DotA*, for example, leveling, three lanes, items, five versus five games, etc. However, even though these games all derived heavily from the same source and were very mechanically similar, there were very few legal problems among all of these companies.

In fact, only one notable lawsuit was filed, and it was for trademark reasons, not copyright. Blizzard, the owner of *Warcraft III: Reign of Chaos*, the game from which the original *DotA* was derived, claimed that Valve could not commercialize the name because it belonged to the Blizzard community and would create confusion as to whether *Dota 2* was a Blizzard product.[46] The end result was that Blizzard conceded to Valve the rights to commercially use *DotA*, and Valve conceded that noncommercial work (the original *DotA*, for instance) could use the *DotA* name freely. To that end, Blizzard changed the name of their game from *Blizzard DotA* to *Blizzard All Stars*, and the final name for the game was *Heroes of the Storm*.

Interestingly enough, sometimes the sponsors of tournaments themselves are selling unlicensed products. A Fighting Game Community (FGC) stream known as TeamSp00ky (sic) is well known in the fighting game community for helping fighting game tournaments with organization, streaming, casting, and other technical assistance.[47] A recent tournament, Winter Brawl X, for which Team Sp00ky provided technical assistance, was sponsored by Hori, The Steam Co., and Dynamic Custom Beadworks.[48] Hori is an online shop for game peripherals, and The Steam Co. sells e-cigarette supplies, but Dynamic Custom Beadworks is interesting because they sell art pieces derived from beads that use copyrighted material.[49] On their seller page on Etsy.com, they state that they are licensed by CAPCOM (the creators of *Street Fighter*[50]) to sell their products. Looking at their product list, for instance, one can see that they also sell Teenage Mutant Ninja Turtles beads, beads based on Nintendo characters, and other franchises that they presumably do not have a license for.

Many phenomena are created by the eSports community that are derivative works but take on a life of their own. Often, these start as inside jokes within the community during a tournament or other eSports function and become fundamental pillars of the community. An interesting question to ask is who owns these rights and who can exploit them? Can the company that owns the game step in and claim rights on these? For example, in the Smash Brothers community, in a tournament on December 6, 2008, a match ended in spectacular fashion and achieved great notoriety due to the energy of the game commentators and the crowd.[51] This was dubbed the "wombo combo" and is now a phrase commonly used by the Smash Brothers community to indicate when a moment is particularly noteworthy and by commentators to rouse the crowd. A brief online search shows that there is substantial "wombo combo"–themed merchandise available, from cups to shirts to phone cases. Some of them only use the text of the commentary, others use silhouettes of the characters from the game, and some others use art assets from the game itself. It would be interesting to see which of these are infringing and which are not. What about the shirt that has the Smash Brothers logo and the words "Wombo Combo." Is that sufficient? Or does it belong to the community, and would the use of the logo be considered incidental?

Two of the biggest eSports titles currently in existence rely heavily on user-generated content as part of their business model. These two games are not coincidentally owned by Valve. In *Dota 2*, players can, through gameplay or payment of money, obtain costumes referred to as "skins" that alter their character's appearance. In *Counter-Strike Global Offensive*,[52] players can also earn through the game or buy "weapon skins," giving the player's in-game weapons a different cosmetic appearance. Although Valve designs and releases a fair number of skins for both games, the vast majority of skins are actually designed by community members and submitted to Valve.[53] Valve then releases the skins they see as high enough quality and sells them in the game, giving a percentage to the creators. Valve announced in 2015 that since the inception of the Steam Workshop in 2011, they had paid out more than $57 million to content creators for their games, with some creators making "six figure salaries."[54] When submitting to the Steam Workshop, creators allow Valve to do what they want with the skins in return for royalties. This means that Valve retains the copyrights to these skins created by the community.

One of the stipulations when submitting a skin to the Steam Workshop is that you state the work is your own and not infringing on another's copyrighted material. This issue came to a head in 2014, when a very popular skin turned out to have been copied from someone else's copyrighted work.[55] Valve made a very clear public statement in which they denounced the action, removed the item from the game, withheld payment from the infringer, and banned the infringer from the game. Many in the community applauded Valve's action for acting on a Digital Millennium Copyright Act (DMCA) claim so quickly and decisively, whereas others worried about potential DMCA abuse threatening content creators' livelihood.

Notes

1. Kelvin Lai contributed to the writing of this chapter.
2. Demmers, Matt. "Leffen Denied Entry to USA for Smash Tournament." *The Score ESports*. N.p., 30 September 2015. Web. 05 Mar. 2016, http://www. thescoreesports.com/news/4122 (Issues for Leffen for Smash); Blum, Bryce. *ESPN*. ESPN Internet Ventures, 02 February 2016. Web. 05 Mar. 2016, http:// espn.go.com/esports/story/_/id/14661486/breaking-league-legends-visa-issue (ESPN article on the issue).
3. Lajaqc, Yannick. "League of Legends Player Tries to Quit Team, Manager Freaks Out." *Kotaku*. N.p., 09 February 2015. Web. 05 Mar. 2016, http://kotaku. com/league-of-legends-player-tries-to-quit-team-manager-fr-1684785833.
4. Lewis, Richard. "How Fair Is an LCS Contract? We Asked a Lawyer." *The Daily Dot*. N.p., 22 September 2014. Web. 05 Mar. 2016, http://www.dailydot. com/esports/lcs-contract-analysis-league-of-legends-riot-games/.
5. "LoL Esports." n.d. Web. 03 Mar. 2016.
6. How Many People Watched Each TI." *Dota 2 News*, October 2008. Web. 03 Mar. 2016.
7. "Essential Facts about the Computer and Video Game Industry." *Boom: A Journal of California* 5.1 (2015): 12–13. Web, http://www.theesa.com/wp-content/ uploads/2015/04/ESA-Essential-Facts-2015.pdf.
8. "Largest Overall Prize Pools in ESports."—*ESports Tournament Rankings*. N.p., n.d. Web. 05 Mar. 2016, http://www.esportsearnings.com/tournaments (judgement based on Tournament prizepool).
9. *Starcraft II*. Blizzard Entertainment. Blizzard Entertainment, 2010. Microsoft Windows, OS X.
10. Grubb, Jeff. "Esports Is Already worth $748M, But It'll Reach $1.9B by 2018." *VentureBeat*. N.p., 28 October 2015. Web. 05 Mar. 2016, http:// venturebeat.com/2015/10/28/analyst-esports-is-already-worth-748m-but-itll-reach-1-9b-by-2018/.
11. *Candy Crush*. King. King, 2012–2015. Multiple platforms.
12. Gaudiosi, John. "This Company Is Hosting the First Ever ESports Event at Madison Square Garden." *Fortune This Company Is Hosting the First Ever ESports Event at Madison Square Garden Comments*. N.p., 09 June 2015. Web. 05 Mar. 2016, http://fortune.com/2015/06/09/riot-games-esports/.
13. Gies, Arthur. "International Dota 2 Championship Prize Pool Reaches $5.5 Million." *Polygon*. N.p., 04 May 2015. Web. 05 Mar. 2016, http:// www.polygon.com/2015/5/4/8545921/international-dota-2-prize-pool-5–5-million-compendium-TI5.

14. "Largest Overall Prize Pools in ESports."—*ESports Tournament Rankings*. N.p., n.d. Web. 05 Mar. 2016, http://www.esportsearnings.com/tournaments.
15. Grubb, Jeff. "Esports Is Already worth $748M, But It'll Reach $1.9B by 2018." *VentureBeat*. N.p., 28 Oct. 2015. Web. 05 Mar. 2016, http://venturebeat.com/2015/10/28/analyst-esports-is-already-worth-748m-but-itll-reach-1–9b-by-2018/.
16. *Street Fighter V*. Capcom/Dimps. Capcom, 2016. Playstation 4, Microsoft Windows, Linux.
17. *Street Fighter IV*. Dimps/Capcom. Capcom, 2008–2015. Multiple platforms.
18. "Evolution Championship Series: E-Sports Earnings." E-Sports Earnings. N.p., n.d. Web. 03 Mar. 2016. http://www.esportsearnings.com/leagues/116-evolution-championship-series
19. *Super Smash Brothers Melee*. HAL Laboratory. Nintendo, 2001–2002. GameCube.
20. *Super Smash Brothers for Wii U*. Sora Ltd./Bandai Namco Games. Nintendo, 2014. Wii U.
21. *Starcraft* (franchise). Blizzard Entertainment. Blizzard Entertainment, 1988–2015. Microsoft Windows, OS X, Nintendo 64.
22. Leahy, Brian. "Blizzard Sues Second Korean Network Over Unlicensed StarCraft: Brood War Broadcasts." *Shacknews*. N.p., November 2010. Web. 03 Mar. 2016. http://www.shacknews.com/article/66360/blizzard-sues-second-korean-network
23. Walker, John. "DRM Is NOTHING Compared to StarCraft II." *Rock Paper Shotgun PC Game Reviews Previews Subjectivity*. N.p., 28 May 2010. Web. 03 Mar. 2016. https://www.rockpapershotgun.com/2010/05/28/drm-is-nothing-compared-to-starcraft-ii/
24. "Korea E-Sports Association." — *Liquipedia*. N.p., n.d. Web. 03 Mar. 2016. http://wiki.teamliquid.net/starcraft2/Korea_e-Sports_Association
25. *Starcraft: Brood War*. Saffire/Blizzard Entertainment. Blizzard Entertainment/Sierra Entertainment, 1998–1999. Windows, Mac OS.
26. "The Entire KeSPA and Blizzard Fiasco in a Nutshell." *Giant Bomb*. N.p., n.d. Web. http://www.giantbomb.com/starcraft-ii-wings-of-liberty/3030-20674/forums/the-entire-kespa-and-blizzard-fiasco-in-a-nutshell-441221/
27. "E-Sports Federation." — *Liquipedia*. N.p., n.d. Web. 03 Mar. 2016. http://wiki.teamliquid.net/starcraft2/E-Sports_Federation
28. "Your Browser Isn't Supported." *YouTube Gaming*. N.p., n.d. Web. 03 Mar. 2016.
29. "Update: Smash Is Back!! Changes to Evo 2013 Smash Schedule." *Shoryuken*. N.p., 09 July 2013. Web. 03 Mar. 2016. http://shoryuken.com/2013/07/09/changes-to-evo-2013-smash-schedule/
30. "The PA Report—The Super Smash Bros. Community Raised Money for Charity and Awareness, and Nintendo." *Penny Arcade*. N.p., n.d. Web. 03 Mar. 2016. https://forums.penny-arcade.com/discussion/180690/the-pa-report-the-super-smash-bros-community-raised-money-for-charity-and-awareness-and-nintendo
31. *Super Smash Brothers Brawl*. Nintendo/Game Arts/Sora Ltd. Nintendo, 2008. Wii.
32. *Project M*. Project M Development Team. 2011. Wii.
33. "Project M." *Wikipedia*. Wikimedia Foundation, n.d. Web. 03 Mar. 2016. https://en.wikipedia.org/wiki/Project_M_(video_game) See also Project M, https://projectmgame.com/.
34. Klepek, Patrick. "The Smash Community Is Chaos Right Now." *Kotaku*. N.p., 03 December 2015. Web. 03 Mar. 2016. http://kotaku.com/the-smash-community-is-chaos-right-now-1746040568

35. Gaudiosi, John. "This ESports Company Just Got Acquired for $87 Million." *Fortune This ESports Company Just Got Acquired for 87 Million Comments.* N.p., 03 July 2015. Web. 05 Mar. 2016, http://fortune.com/2015/07/03/esl-esports-acquisition/.
36. *Heroes of the Storm.* Blizzard Entertainment. Blizzard Entertainment, 2015. Microsoft Windows, OS X.
37. *Hearthstone: Heroes of Warcraft.* Blizzard Entertainment. Blizzard Entertainment, 2014–2015. Microsoft Windows, OS X, iOS, Android.
38. *Splatoon.* Nintendo EAD. Nintendo, 2015. Wii U.
39. "For All the People Who Keep Asking If Nintendo Made Any Announcements at Apex, They Did Not. It Was an Awards Ceremony for Community Members before Melee Top 8. • /r/smashbros." *Reddit.* N.p., n.d. Web. 05 Mar. 2016, https://www.reddit.com/r/smashbros/comments/2uk7c1/for_all_the_people_who_keep_asking_if_nintendo/.
40. "Jxself.org." *What Can Be Copyrighted and What Can't.* N.p., n.d. Web. 05 Mar. 2016, https://jxself.org/what-can-be-copyrighted-and-what-cant.shtml.
41. "U.S. Copyright Office—Games." *U.S. Copyright Office—Games.* N.p., n.d. Web. 05 Mar. 2016, http://www.copyright.gov/fls/fl108.html.
42. *Heroes of Newerth.* S2 Games/Frostburn Studios. Frostburn Studios, 2010. Microsoft Windows, OS X, Linux.
43. *Smite.* H-Rez Studios. Hi-Rez Studios, 2014–2015. Microsoft Windows, Playstation 4, Xbox One.
44. *Warcraft III: Reign of Chaos.* Blizzard Entertainment. Blizzard Entertainment, 2002. Microsoft Windows, Mac OS.
45. *Wikipedia.* Wikimedia Foundation, n.d. Web. 05 Mar. 2016, https://en.wikipedia.org/wiki/Heroes_of_Newerth.
46. Haas, Pete. "Blizzard, Valve Settle DOTA Lawsuit | CINEMABLEND." *Blizzard, Valve Settle DOTA Lawsuit.* N.p., 12 May 2012. Web. 05 Mar. 2016, http://www.cinemablend.com/games/Blizzard-Valve-Settle-DOTA-Lawsuit-42430.html.
47. "TeamSp00ky." *Twitch.* N.p., n.d. Web. 05 Mar. 2016, http://www.twitch.tv/teamsp00ky, information in their channel description.
48. Walker, Ian. "Winter Brawl X Results." *SRK.* N.p. February 2016, http://shoryuken.com/2016/02/28/winter-brawl-x-streaming-live-from-essington-pennsylvania/; https://www.facebook.com/teamspooky/, in posts dated for 2–28–16.
49. "DCBPerlerSprites." *Etsy.* N.p., n.d. Web. 05 Mar. 2016, https://www.etsy.com/shop/DCBPerlerSprites?page=1.
50. *Street Fighter* (franchise). Capcom. Capcom, 1987–2016. Multiple platforms.
51. "Wombo Combo." *Know Your Meme News.* N.p., n.d. Web. 05 Mar. 2016, http://knowyourmeme.com/memes/wombo-combo.
52. *Counter-Strike: Global Offensive.* Hidden Path Entertainment/Value Corporation. Valve Corporation, 2012. Multiple platforms.
53. "About Workshop: Here's How It Works." *Steam Workshop.* Valve, n.d. Web. 03 Mar. 2016. https://steamcommunity.com/workshop/workshopsubmitinfo/
54. O'Connor, Alice. "Over $57 Million Paid Out to Steam Workshop Creators." *Rock Paper Shotgun.* N.p., 30 January 2015. Web. 03 Mar. 2016. https://www.rockpapershotgun.com/2015/01/30/steam-workshop-57-million-dollars/
55. Savage, Phil. "Counter Strike: Global Offensive Weapon Skin Removed After DMCA Takedown Notice." *PC Gamer.* N.p., 11 June 2014. Web. 03 Mar. 2016. http://www.pcgamer.com/counter-strike-global-offensive-weapon-skin-removed-after-dmca-takedown-notice/

7 Conclusion
The New Normal[1]

The Video Game Bar Association's website declares: "Video games have become the new normal in media as television and movies were in the past."[2] In the summer of 2016, *Pokémon Go* carried us one more step into the "new normal." To conclude this work, we look briefly at *Pokémon Go*, as indicative both of the expansion of video games into ever-wider spaces of culture and of the myriad legal issues that has accompanied this expansion.

Pokémon Go and Augmented Reality

Pokémon Go is a free-to-play, location-based, augmented reality (AR) game developed by Niantic for IOS and Android devices. It was released worldwide in July 2016. It uses your phone's global positioning system (GPS) and clock to detect your location and make Pokémon characters appear on your phone screens.[3] The idea is to encourage users to physically travel around to catch Pokémon in different areas. It is so popular that it is now competing with Twitter in terms of active daily users around the world.[4] As of July 13, 2016, *Pokémon Go* was the biggest mobile game in U.S. history to be released since *Candy Crush Saga*. More than 20 million people downloaded the game in its first week of release.[5] Since then, downloads have peaked at 45 million, and although these figures are declining, the game continues to be extremely popular worldwide.[6]

In order to understand *Pokémon Go* and the legal issues surrounding it, we must first examine the concepts driving the game. Augmented reality refers to a view of the physical, real-world environment whose elements are supplemented or augmented with computer-generated images and sound via an electronic device.[7] In *Pokémon Go*'s case, streets, parks, and the entire world have been augmented with a Google Map interface, playing home to Pokémon creatures, battle gymnasiums, and Pokéstops.[8]

Three companies are involved. The Pokémon Company, the creator of the Pokémon universe, has copyrighted and trademarked works known all over the world. Originally launching *Pokémon* in Japan as early as 1996, The Pokémon Company is responsible for the mass marketing, licensing, and brand management and protection of their augmented reality world.[9] Niantic, Inc., the company behind the previous augmented reality application, Ingress, decided to release another game in the form of *Pokémon Go*. According to some sources who have researched the intellectual property aspects of the developer's global craze,[10] Niantic, Inc., has two patents: a provisional patent filed in 2012 and a utility patent filed in 2013. The patent was recently issued in December 2015. Nintendo filed its trademark applications for *Pokémon Go* in March.[11] Nintendo will only continue to grow its Pokémon universe by bringing more of its graphics, sounds, and products into this smartphone world.

Since its release, *Pokémon Go* has helped thousands of small businesses grow.[12] The same 'lures' and 'baits' within the game used by robbers and criminals to commit crimes are also being used by businesses to attract players. Some of these players subsequently become customers of the stores. Some businesses have become lucky in that they have been randomly selected by the software engineers and creators of the game as a 'Pokéstop'.[13] Brick-and-mortar businesses have been placing signage, advertising their in-game location to drive players to their stores and generate revenue.[14] In addition to out-of-game advertising, businesses are adding 'Lure Modules' to their in-game location, causing players to flock to their stores to catch the Pokémon.[15] The 'Lure Module Technique'[16] costs businesses $1.19 per hour while the business is open. Sales for these businesses often increase dramatically, making it a very cheap revenue-generating technique.[17]

Niantic CEO John Hanke said that "sponsored locations" would provide a new revenue stream in addition to in-app purchases of power-ups and virtual items.[18] Put simply, retailers and companies will be granted the paid opportunity to be featured prominently on the game's virtual map in the hope to drive customers inside their facilities.[19] Some commentators have suggested large global corporations like McDonald's have already initiated discussions with Niantic for a potential in-game sponsorship.[20] It would work similar to the "cost per click" system used in Google's search advertising.[21]

Legal Issues

Does placing an AR element, that is, a Pokémon creature or item, or even transferring a location or item into a Pokéstop without the property owner's consent, affect the exclusive right to possession of his or her property?[22]

All property owners have a 'bundle of rights' in their property.[23] The most well-known is the exclusive right of possession. By placing these AR elements and objects into another's property without the consent of the property owner, the developers have now affected all property owners residing in the United States and abroad, including the exclusive rights in their own property as against others.[24]

For example, people are now wandering into other people's private property looking for Pokémon to catch or places to catch these creatures. These actions could constitute what is described as trespass. Trespass is an injury to possession. It is a tort committed when one, without permission, interferes with or invades a possessor's protected interest in exclusive possession.[25] The term "intrusion" denotes that a possessor's interest in the exclusive possession of his or her land has been invaded by the presence of a person or thing upon it without the possessor's consent.[26]

Trespass is an affirmative act interfering with possessory rights. To constitute a trespass, there must be an unlawful physical invasion of the property or possession of another.[27] Although AR objects aren't 'real' and don't constitute a physical invasion of property, an intangible invasion to property may occur. To recover in trespass for an *intangible invasion* to property, a plaintiff must show (1) an invasion affecting an interest in exclusive possession; (2) the act resulting in the invasion was intentional; (3) reasonable foreseeability that the act could result in an invasion of the plaintiff's possessory interest; and (4) substantial damage to the property.[28] This analysis applies to the creators and companies behind the *Pokémon Go* game.

In addition, many stories of physical invasions to property have surfaced by users chasing Pokémon. These property invasions are illegal if not authorized by the private owner. Users may also subject themselves to danger and run the risk of serious injury while chasing these Pokémon. These players often illegally enter unknown private property and expose themselves to unknown threats.

Developers and users of the *Pokémon Go* app have also attracted publicity for the number of dangerous and sometimes deadly situations that have surfaced since its release. News stories around the world have shown numerous people targeting players using the application's geolocation feature. In some cases, robbers have lured unwitting victims into specific areas where they are known to congregate for 'battles and team hunts.'[29] These criminals are able to lure victims by dropping baits in certain locations.[30]

In the game's terms of service, Niantic explicitly states that you should

> be aware of your surroundings and play safely. You agree that your use of the App and play of the game is at your own risk, and it is your

responsibility to maintain such health, liability, hazard, personal injury, medical, life, and other insurance policies as you deem reasonably necessary for any injuries that you may incur while using the services.[31]

Interestingly, it may be the only game available in the App Store to suggest an insurance policy for players of the game.[32] This may actually be necessary, considering some players are falling off cliffs while playing the game.[33] This alone should make users realize that playing the game may increase the likelihood of sustaining injuries.

Pokémon demonstrates the wide impact of video gaming in our world. Although its user base is declining, *Pokémon Go* remains a revolutionary augmented reality game capable of changing the nature of the video game industry, its interaction with people, and the law. The laws must adapt to these types of games and ensure people and property are properly protected into the future. Although there is a plethora of potential business opportunities, owners should comply with laws and be aware of the risks associated with increased exposure and traffic.

Overall, video games have continuously raised copyright and other legal questions since their debut as a new interactive form of media. As technology continues to advance, so do the possibilities and complexities of the video gaming industry. Games today do not merely exist as cartridges people play alone in their living rooms. Modern game consoles like the Xbox One, Wii U, and PlayStation 4 allow for the possibility of online play. Downloadable games remove the need for a physical copy of the game and utilize end user licensing agreements and digital rights management methods that raise legal questions regarding the first sale doctrine.[34]

As the video game industry continues to grow and becomes more mainstream, the fan community also continues to grow, finding inventive ways to share and enjoy their video gaming experiences. The matters presented thus far are merely an introduction to the complex and ever-changing world of video game intellectual property issues. It is clear that 'Let's Plays' live within the legal grey area that is fair use. As has been shown, arguments exist to permit the use of the gameplay within these types of videos, and a number of developers expressly state their support for such videos. However, this could all change if this support was to be withdrawn or if a court were to decide that the use is not transformative in nature. And as we see with *Pokémon Go*, the legal issues and business opportunities go far beyond the game itself. Trespass, criminal liability, robbery, and physical injuries are added to the list of issues arising from video games.

As we interviewed attorneys in the gaming field, they all had stories of how the industry grew up over the last thirty years and how they had to invent and think through elements like user-generated content relationships and eSports, as well as use conventional tools of licensing and other trans-actional tools for manufacturing, third-party gaming, and merchandise deals. Patrick Sweeney, an attorney for over 140 video game clients, said of his practice that it was horizontal in subject—you need to know a lot of different areas and how they fit within the gaming world.[35]

The video game industry has particularly interesting legal issues. Many more are the same as any business—noncompete clauses for employees, contract issues, and other day-to-day legal questions. This book sought to provide an overview of the legal issues that arise from the creative process.

Notes

1. John Billiris contributed to the writing of this chapter.
2. Video Game Bar Association, https://vgba.org/
3. German Lopez, *Pokémon Go, Explained*, Vox, August 5, 2016, 8:50 am, http://www.vox.com/2016/7/11/12129162/pokemon-go-android-ios-game.
4. Ibid.
5. Allan, Robbie. "Pokémon Go Statistics Say It's the Biggest Mobile Game in U.S. History." *Survey Monkey*, 13 July 2016, https://www.surveymonkey.com/business/intelligence/pokemon-go-biggest-mobile-game-ever/
6. Kawa, L., and L. Katz. "These Charts Show That Pokémon Go Is Already in Decline." *Bloomberg Markets*, August 22, 2016, 12:19 pm, http://www.bloomberg.com/news/articles/2016–08–22/these-charts-show-that-pokemon-go-is-already-in-decline.
7. Wassom, Brian. "Pokémon Go and the Crisis on an Infinitely Augmented Earth." Wassom, 10 July 2016, http://www.wassom.com/6316.html.
8. Rosso, Andrew L. "Gotta Catch. . .A Lawsuit? A Legal Insight into the Bat-tlefield Pokémon Go Has Downloaded onto Smartphones and Properties around the World." *Ohio Bar Association*, 20 July 2016, https://www.ohiobar.org/NewsAndPublications/News/OSBANews/Pages/Gotta-catch-a-lawsuit-A-legal-insight-into-the-battlefield-Pokemon-Go-has-downloaded-onto-smart phones-and-properties.aspx#_ftn5.
9. Ibid.
10. Crockett, Susan L. "Supporting Pokémon With Intellectual Property." http://www.crockett-crockett.com/supporting-pokemon-intellectual-property/
11. Ibid.
12. Roemmele, Brian. "How to Ride the Pokémon Go Wave to Success." *Forbes*, 22 July 2016, 4:21 pm, http://www.forbes.com/sites/quora/2016/07/22/how-to-ride-the-pokemon-wave-to-business-success/#651514742063.
13. Tompkins, Matt. "Lure Customers with these Pokémon Go Marketing Strategies." *Vert*, July 15, 2016, http://vertdigital.com/blog/lure-customers-pokemon-go-marketing-strategies/
14. Ibid.
15. Ibid.
16. Roemmele, Brian. "How to Ride the Pokémon Go Wave to Success." *Forbes*, 22 July 2016, 4:21pm, http://www.forbes.com/sites/quora/2016/07/22/how-to-ride-the-pokemon-wave-to-business-success/#651514742063.

17. Whitten, Sarah. "Gotta Catch 'em All: Pokémon Go Is Boosting Business for Restaurants." *CNBC*, July 12, 2016, 11:40 am, http://www.cnbc.com/2016/07/12/gotta-catch-em-all-pokemon-go-is-boosting-business-for-restaurants.html.
18. Maffei, Lucia. "PokémonGoWillSoonGetAdsintheFormofSponsoredLocations." *Tech Crunch*, 13 July 2016, https://techcrunch.com/2016/07/13/pokemon-go-will-soon-get-ads-in-the-form-of-sponsored-locations/
19. Ibid.
20. Menegus, Brian. "It Looks like Pokémon Go Is Pursuing a Partnership with McDonald's." *Gizmodo*, July 13, 2016, 10:13 am, http://gizmodo.com/it-looks-like-pokemon-go-is-pursuing-a-partnership-with-1783580645.
21. Ibid.
22. Weiss, Debra Cassens. "Pokémon Go Spurs Lawyers to Stop and Consider Legal Issues." *ABA Journal*, July 13, 2016, 8:00 am, http://www.abajournal.com/news/article/pokemon_go_spurs_lawyers_to_stop_and_consider_legal_issues.
23. Ibid.
24. Ibid.
25. Lee, Keith. "Is PokemonGo Illegal?" *Associates Mind*, 13 July 2016, http://associatesmind.com/2016/07/11/is-pokemongo-illegal/
26. Ibid.
27. Dickie's Sportsman's Centers, Inc. v. Dep't of Transp. & Dev., 477 So. 2d 744, 750 (La. Ct. App. 1985).
28. Borland v. Sanders Lead Co., Inc., 369 So. 2d 523, 2 A.L.R.4th 1042 (Ala. 1979).
29. CBS News, "'Pokémon Go' Being Used to Stage Robberies." *Police Say*, 10 July 2016, 10:29 am, http://www.cbsnews.com/news/robbery-suspects-using-pokemon-go-to-target-victims-police-say/
30. Reuters, "Wildly Popular Pokémon Go Leads to Robberies." *Injuries and a Body*, 12 July 2016, 8:4 am, http://fortune.com/2016/07/12/pokemon-go-injuries-robberies/
31. Carl Brooks Jnr., "The Pokémon Go Injuries Are Already Piling Up." *The Ringer*, 08 July 2016, https://theringer.com/pokemon-go-injuries-already-piling-up-250ec4c150bd#.yjxcjaljv.
32. Ibid.
33. Rocha, Veronica. "2 California Men Fall Off Edge of Ocean Bluff While Playing Pokémon Go." *Los Angeles Times*, 14 July 2016, 3:45 pm, http://www.latimes.com/local/lanow/la-me-ln-pokemon-go-players-stabbed-fall-off-cliff-20160714-snap-story.html.
34. "Xbox 360 Digital Rights Management." *Digital Rights Management*. Microsoft, n.d. Web. 03 Mar. 2016, http://support.xbox.com/en-US/xbox-360/store/download-content.
35. Sweeney, Patrick. Interview, http://ielawgroup.net/patrick-sweeney/.

Index

Printed in the United States
by Baker & Taylor Publisher Services